# *And Then We Were Women*

Three small portions of this book have appeared in print before. Sections from chapter 2 originally appeared in *Today's Christian Woman* (March/April 1992), sections from chapter 10 originally appeared in *Moody Monthly* (February 1992), and sections from chapter 11 originally appeared in *Moody Monthly* (February 1989).

# And Then We Were Women

❖

## Dee Brestin

While this book is intended for the reader's personal
enjoyment and profit, it is also designed for group study.
A leader's guide with Reproducible Response Sheets is
available from your local bookstore or from the publisher.

VICTOR BOOKS

A DIVISION OF SCRIPTURE PRESS PUBLICATIONS INC.
USA CANADA ENGLAND

Copyediting: Jane Vogel; Barbara Williams
Cover Design: Grace Chan Mallette
Cover Painting: Dan Barsness

---

**Library of Congress Cataloging-in-Publication Data**

Brestin, Dee, 1944–
    And then we were women / Dee Brestin.
        p.      cm.
    Includes bibliographical references.
    1. Women — Religious life. 2. Women — Psychology. I. Title.
BV4527.B686 1994
248.8'43 — dc20                                                      94-11827
                                                                         CIP

---

1  2  3  4  5  6  7  8  9  10  Printing / Year  98  97  96  95  94

## OTHER TITLES BY DEE BRESTIN

*The Friendships of Women* (Victor)
Accompanying Leader's Guide available
*The Lifestyles of Christian Women* (Victor)
Accompanying Leader's Guide available
*The Joy of Hospitality* (Victor)
*The Joy of Eating Right* (Victor)
*The Joy of Women's Friendships* (Victor)

Fisherman Bible studyguides (Harold Shaw Publishers)
*Proverbs and Parables*
*Ecclesiastes*
*Examining the Claims of Christ* (John 1–5)
*1, 2 Peter and Jude*
*How Should a Christian Live* (1, 2, 3 John)
*Higher Ground*
*Building Your House on the Lord: Marriage and Parenthood*
*Friendship: Portraits from God's Family Album*

*To my big sisters,*
*Sally Brown Frahm and*
*Bonnie Brown Rock.*
*You are still my mentors.*

# Acknowledgments

I did not write this book alone. I needed the eyes, the hearts, and the hands of my sisters and brothers in Christ. Though you are many, there are a few I wish to mention by name.

Greg Clouse, at Victor Books, spent hours with me on the phone, listening, brainstorming, responding. Often he would disclaim, "But what do I know? I'm a man. And this is a woman's book!" (Yet your insights were uncanny, Greg! I suspect you are a rare right-brained male!) It was Greg who titled this book, drawing on one of my headings. And I know Greg would turn around and acknowledge the staff at Victor—for he often drew on *their* giftedness. He took the proposed cover painting (by Dan Barsness—who also deserves a thank-you!) to the women at Victor and then called me to enthusiastically report: "The response is 100 percent!" And it was Greg who led me to work with two very gifted people: editor Jane Vogel and cartoonist Steve Bjorkman.

Two pairs of sisters were of enormous help: Cynthia Clawson and her younger sister, Patti Clawson Berry; and Carol Kent and her younger sister, Jennie Dimkoff. Thank you for being so open with me about your relationship as sisters!

A thank-you to my friends, including my sisters, for their support and help. And finally, I am particularly thankful to my precious family. A special thank-you to my daughter Sally for her illustrations in chapter 4 and to my husband, Steve, for reading every page and every rewritten page and giving me his priceless input.

# Contents

*Women friends strengthen one another's marriages by participating in what researchers call "marriage work."*

one
# Marriage Work

During times of crisis the brain releases a chemical which indelibly imprints the details of that experience on your memory. Perhaps that's why, though it's been twenty-five years, that I can picture that morning as if it were yesterday.

Three-year-old J.R., clad in a blue Sears Winnie-the-Pooh sleeper and an Indian headdress, pranced around Johnny, who was bouncing in his jumper seat, waving his chubby baby arms, enticing his brother into faster and faster circles.

My merry sons were oblivious to my mood, which matched the gloomy Seattle skies. Seated at my husband's desk, surrounded by medical books and unpaid bills, I stared out at the heavy mist blanketing the Puget Sound, listening to foghorns bellowing deep, long warnings to other freighters slipping past on a November morn. After the fight we'd had last night, why hadn't Steve called?

In the five months since we'd moved from Indianapolis, I'd barely seen Steve. A medical internship is often the worst year of medical training, where doctors and residents take advantage of the lowly intern, piling work on him. Many a medical marriage has died during that lethal year — and ours was definitely ailing.

Two years earlier Steve and I had come to faith in Christ, but we were young, and so was our faith, like a fragile sapling facing winds of hurricane strength. The previous night Steve had been home for one hour before he returned for all-night call — and we'd spent that precious hour fighting. Or rather, I'd spent that hour crying and accusing Steve of abandoning us. Steve had listened, his face weary, his deep blue eyes troubled. And then, glancing sadly at me and our two precious boys, he'd slipped out the door, without a promise of resolution.

After a restless night, I was eager to have our conflict resolved. Steve had always been the strong, resourceful one in our marriage. Why hadn't he called?

Finally, at 8 A.M., the phone rang. I'll never forget that conversation — or my husband's emotional state. Haltingly, he began: "I wanted to call you with the promise that things would be better." He paused. "I hoped I could tell you we'd have some time as a family over the holidays." Another long pause. "I just saw the schedule. I'm working on Thanksgiving, Christmas Eve, and Christmas."

Disappointment filled my heart — but before I could complain, a crisis much bigger than forsaken holidays loomed. For the first time I heard my husband break down. His sobs — so foreign to my ears — frightened me. Finally he gained enough control to say four words, words which stopped my heart: "I'm willing to quit."

I froze, my body rigid, my mouth silenced — but my thoughts raced: *Quit — now? After four difficult years of medical school? After moving across the country? Did he mean it?* Yes, I knew he did! *I* might say something like that in order to manipulate him, but Steve wouldn't. My dad had helped us through medical school. What would he think? QUIT? How could we? But if we didn't . . . could we make it?

Again, with our situation unresolved, Steve had to go. We were both in tears when we hung up. And, as people often do when they feel like cornered rabbits, we each cried out to God for help.

## A little help from my friends

J.R. began to fuss because I hadn't let him talk to his daddy, and suddenly I felt propelled into action. I told J.R. we were going to catch a bus, and his face brightened. "Bus!" he repeated excitedly.

A young mothers' Bible study met on Thursday mornings, but I hadn't wanted to go alone, hadn't had the courage to ask someone to pick me up. Now I dressed the boys hurriedly, stuffed them into their snowsuits, put Johnny in his stroller, and raced with J.R.'s mittened hand in mine to the top of Magnolia Hill. The bus came into sight as we neared the stop and we waved frantically at the driver. He hopped off and helped me with Johnny's stroller — an act of gallantry, an evidence of God's grace. Then we rolled up and down hills until we came to the bottom of Queen Anne Hill, just a block from the church. I deposited the boys in the nursery and climbed the stairs to an hour that changed my life. I didn't utter one word that morning, but when my turn came for prayer requests, the tears spilled over. I couldn't believe I was crying in front of a group of strangers and I couldn't stop!

A few women came and put their arms around me. A few prayed for me. And afterward, the invitations began to come: for lunch, for coffee, for a walk around Green Lake with our kids.

## Women's friendships and their marriages

I've been fascinated by studies showing the impact of women's friendships on the family. What makes these studies particularly intriguing is that they are studies of women who do not necessarily have a personal walk with God. Yet even for these women the evidence is overwhelming that women's friendships help rather than hurt marriages.

C. Goodenow, professor at Tufts University, and E.L. Gaier, professor at the University of New York at Buffalo, found that married women who had one or more close, reciprocal friendships were significantly less depressed, more satisfied with their lives, and had higher self-esteem than those who did not have such a friendship.[1] Women like this are more likely to have happy marriages.

A study in the *American Journal of Sociology* by Arlie Hochschild[2] showed that women, when they are empathetic about marital troubles, help their women friends undergo a "frame change," similar to the cartoon in the opening of this chapter. As women recounted these frame changes, their voices carried awe and appreciation for the friends who moved them from anger and negativity to affection and hope.

An extensive study by S.J. Oliker[3] found that women's friendships promote marital stability because they meet intimacy needs which are not met by marriage, and they help diffuse anger and other volatile emotions.

You might think that when a husband and wife have a quarrel, the wife's friend would support her grievance and strategize with her friend to help her get her way. One man expressed his fears concerning his wife's close friendships like this: "If Ginny and I have a fight and she runs to see Lori — of course Lori's going to take Ginny's side. She's Ginny's best friend! They're going to run me through the meat grinder!"

But Oliker found that, rather than siding with the wife against the husband, a woman is much more likely to participate in what she calls "marriage work," endeavoring to strengthen her friend's marriage by helping her to see the situation from his perspective, by "framing" the husband in such a way as to "enoble him," or by diffusing her anger with humor. Here are a few intriguing testimonies Oliker has heard:

> So much of the time I only see my side — I've got blinders on. And June will say, "You know, he's probably feeling real insecure and angry." And for the first time I'll realize there's another human being mixed up in this, instead of just me and my own passions.

> Occasionally, my friends will say something about Jeff that puts him in a different light and makes me appreciate him more. He impresses people in certain ways that I forget because I live with it. Like someone will mention something he said that went right past me. And I'll think, "That's kind of nice."

> Doreen tells me, "Jesse loves you." And he's this and he's that. She tells me his fine points and puts me in good spirits about him.[4]

This is exactly the kind of help I experienced that volatile year in Seattle from the women friends I'd met at Bible study. Patti told me how evident it was to her that Steve loved me and the boys. "He keeps his arm around you whenever you're together! And his eyes light up when he's talking about the boys!''

And I thought, ''That's true. I *am* blessed.''

And Lorinda, who also had two little boys, helped me laugh about the trials and tribulations of being housebound with two small males. One day I called Lorinda in near hysteria because J.R. had dragged the baby by the ankle down the hall to a bath I was preparing for him. All I had heard was the clunk, clunk, clunk of Johnny's head as it bumped along the hardwood floor of the long hall and I had wondered, ''What could that noise be?'' (Johnny *was* crying— but it was a desperate, silent cry.) When I realized that the clunk had been my precious infant's head, I lost it! I screamed at my terrified toddler as I cradled Johnny. Imagining permanent brain damage, I tried to call Steve, but he was in surgery. Remembering Lorinda was a nurse, I frantically called her and poured out my story. Calmly she asked me if Johnny was vomiting, or dazed, or sleepy. When I replied negatively to all her inquiries, she paused, and then she began to laugh softly.

''I'm sorry to laugh, Dee! But I'm sure Johnny's going to be just fine.'' She giggled again. ''Poor little J.R.! He thought he was helping. And he was being obedient, because you told him not to pick the baby up!'' Now I was smiling.

''I wish I could have seen your face when you realized the clunk, clunk, clunk was Johnny's head,'' Lorinda continued. ''I would have died if that was Keith dragging Cullen!''

And so, what had seemed like a tragedy just twenty minutes earlier, now had us both laughing. Lorinda helped me to see the humor, and my tension and anger at my innocent toddler was gone. (And Johnny was not brain-damaged— he's been at the top of his class all his life.)

Before I joined the young mothers' Bible study, I felt as if I were swimming the English Channel with two little boys on my back—and we were sinking! But the emotional support I received from my new friends was like a lifeline that not only enabled us to survive, but also to give Steve the understanding and love he so desperately needed in his grueling internship.

*I'm so thankful God used my friends to help our marriage survive Steve's internship so that our sons, J.R. (the older) and Johnny, could grow up in an undivided home.*

Women's friendships generally strengthen marriages, but there are exceptions! For example, one young woman said, "My husband is a couch potato. If I try to talk to him, he grunts. So, every night I go across the street and spend a few hours talking to my friend Judy. Her husband is just as much of a jerk — so she understands."

Rather than participating in Oliker's "marriage work," these two women are helping each other chip away at their marriages, like the woman in Proverbs 14:1, who "with her own hands tears her house down." I'll be examining the dangers of some friendships later, but for now it's important to see the link between spiritual maturity and helping one another to become the wives, mothers, sisters, and women God longs for us to be.

*Wow! Not where we need to be as Christian women.*

**17**

## Driven to connect

Sociologists tell us that the primary drive for women is connection, whereas the primary drive for men is status. Spiritual maturity tempers these drives in both sexes.

Psychiatrist Jean Baker Miller of Wellesley College's Stone Center explains that the terror for women is isolation. Their sense of worth is grounded in the ability to make and maintain relationships. When women attempt suicide, it is usually because of failures involving lovers, family, or friends.[5] This drive for connection can be good when tempered with maturity, but cruel when it is not.

The easiest way to understand the problems caused by immaturity is by observing little girls. Little girls are territorial, and can become treacherous if they feel their best friendship is threatened. Kim, a sixth grader, wrote to Tess, the new girl in school. Kim was angry because Tess had made overtures of friendship toward Kim's best friend. When Tess arrived at school one September morning, she found an envelope taped to her locker. On the front was typed:

IMPORTANT INSTRUCTIONS FOR TESS:
READ IMMEDIATELY!

Tess tore open the envelope:

> Dear Tess:
> Stay away from Emily. *Emily is my best friend.* You are trespassing. Don't save Emily a seat at lunch. Don't wait for her at her locker. Don't give her notes in the hall. Emily is my best friend and you must find a different best friend. Stay away!!!
>     Is that clear?
>
> Love,
>
> Kim

This demanding possessiveness is not too different from

the immaturity that I demonstrated in Seattle when I expected my husband to be all things to me. As women mature, they usually find more than one source with whom to
connect — a married woman will connect with her husband
and a few good woman friends. However, the healthiest
change occurs if a woman matures spiritually and learns
how to depend on God. She still treasures and nurtures her
human relationships, but her dependence shifts toward the
One who will never move away, or betray her, or die. This
transfer of trust from people to God doesn't happen all at
once — and won't be completed until she sees Christ face-to-
face. But it is facilitated when her primary connections have
the wisdom to help her find strength in God rather than in
themselves.

GOD

Secular women are not equipped to help each other find
strength in God, but Christian women are, if they will just
use their resources! The women friends I met in the Seattle
Bible study that life-changing year helped me *begin* the long
process of maturing in Christ, of making my *primary connection* to Him, so that my other connections could be
healthy.

Patti and Lorinda, my closest Seattle friends, both had a
deep faith in God. When we were together, we discussed
Christian books we were reading, or Scriptures we were trying to understand, or adventures in our journey of faith. As
young women together, we helped each other explore our
challenging roles as godly wives and mothers. When things
were troubling us in our marriages, we provided a release
for each other, but we also helped each other believe the best
about our husbands, because we knew marriage was sacred
in God's eyes. The spiritual dimension of our friendship
helped us begin the process of transferring our dependence
from people to God. As women mature in Christ, they become less clinging in their relationships. They become more
like Christ, who, though He treasured His earthly friends,

was willing to let them go in order to be obedient to His Father.

## Driven toward status

The primary drive for men, sociologists tell us, is status, rather than connection. If a man attempts suicide, it's commonly over an injured sense of pride or competence, a perceived loss of status – often related to work.[6]

The female drive for connection and the male drive for status are polar opposites. One of the reasons men find it so difficult to be intimate is that the risks one must take (making oneself vulnerable, expressing love, asking for help) all potentially threaten status.

Even our conversations show our differing drives. Women, who long to connect, will draw one another out in conversation and trade confidences. That was the way Patti, Lorinda, and I conversed. When our three husbands were with us as well, we often felt left out of the conversation, because they would hold the floor and monologue, telling stories or jokes in order to achieve status.

As men mature spiritually, they become less concerned about status, because they find their status in Christ. As that happens, they also become less afraid of intimacy. They become like Christ, who was willing to make Himself vulnerable, express emotion, and ask for help. Small male accountability and prayer groups and movements like Promise-Keepers are helping men mature and become the men God longs for them to be.

## Maturity and fruitfulness

Jesus became angry with the fig tree that, year after year, failed to produce fruit. It should have been bearing fruit, but it failed to mature. Its life, its purpose for being, was wasted.

Likewise, Jesus longs for us to mature and bear fruit. If we are slow to grow up, or if we never grow up at all, we miss priceless opportunities for impacting others for good. The sooner we can mature, the more plentiful the seasons of fruitfulness in our lives.

In this book, we will be looking at how the friendships of women impact the family, but also at the friendships of women within the family: mothers and daughters, sisters, and the volatile relationship of an ex-wife and a new wife. Scripture abounds with models of female relationships that impact the family, models through which God longs to teach us so that we can become women of excellence before too many seasons of potential fruitfulness pass us by.

I am excited to begin this journey with you!

# Bible Study for Individuals or Small Groups

Meditate on the following passages during your daily time alone with the Lord. Look for commands, comparisons, key phrases, and words. *Write down as many observations as you can.* An example of recording observations on a didactic passage is given in the Bible study notes at the back of the book. (A leader's guide with additional helps is available for those who wish to study this book with a small group.)

Proverbs 14:1

Observations:

Meaning:

Application:

Luke 1:39-45 and 56. (Good questions to ask in a narrative passage are *Where? When? Who? What? How?* and *Why?*) An example of recording observations on a narrative passage is given at the end of this book.

Observations:

Principles to apply:

Application:

Mark 11:12-14

Observations:

Principles to apply:

Application:

# Part I

**When I was a child,
I spoke like a child,
I reasoned like a child....**

1 Corinthians 13:11 (NRSVB)

*Actual conversation by nine-year-old*
*Matthew Patton of North Carolina*
*with his mother, Deanna Patton.*

## two
# The Way We Were

We were at the lake, and Barbara arrived, as she always
does, with flamboyance. I was out on the water on a large
anchored wooden raft, teaching my daughters, Sally and
Anne, how to do back dives. Barbara's whoops of greeting
echoed across the bay.

"HELLOOO! HELLOOO! I AM HAPPEEEE TO BE IN

EPHRAIM! YES! YES! IT IS GOOD! HELLOOO MY FAM-
ILY! HELLOOOOOOOOOOO!!!'' Anne, then eight, whom
we'd adopted two years before from an orphanage in Korea,
had never met Barbara. Mesmerized, Anne stood up slowly
and squinted at the woman hollering on the shore: ''Mom,
who is that lady?''

Sally and I exchanged knowing smiles.

Enthusiastically, I explained, ''Annie, you are about to
meet Barbara!'' I held up two fingers, pressed tightly
together, ''She and I were like this growing up!''

I waved both arms heartily to Barbara who waved back
and whooped, ''OHHHHHH, DEE DEE!''

I dove in, with Sally following. Anne, bundled in a bright
orange life-preserver, leapt after us. Effie, our springer
spaniel, a flying mass of black-and-white fur, jumped too.

Barbara bounded down the hill, crying, ''MY SISTER
DEE DEE, MY SISTER DEE DEE!'' She plunged into
Green Bay and swam toward us. When we met, she scooped
me up, whirled me around, and whooped: ''YOUR MAID OF
HONOR HAS ARRIVED!''

Anne's astonished face caused Barbara to burst into
laughter, drop me, and duck under the water. Anne
screamed as she found herself rising from the water on Barbara's shoulders. Barbara shouted, ''This can only be AN-
NIE! ANNIE, ANNIE, ANNIE — what a PRECIOUS DAR-
LING you are! And SALLY,'' she looked unabashedly at
Sally's blossoming breasts, ''you are becoming a WOMAN!''

Many of the friends Barbara and I have made as adults
are surprised by the intimacy of our friendship, for today
Barbara and I are a study in contrasts.

Barbara considers herself an ''Earth Mother,'' living in
the mountains of Oregon in a sleeping shelter she built with
friends. She dresses like a hippie from the 1960s, in long
flowing dresses and Indian jewelry, her shining black hair
braided to her waist, her feet perennially bare. For the last

seven years she has lived and traveled around the world
with a much younger man, named Craig. They plan to stay
together as long as they give each other "good energy." Barbara practices yoga in her backyard, floats down the Rogue
River in an inner tube, and celebrates the summer and
winter solstices. As a child, she enjoyed shocking people – and
she still does. Watching my children's eyes widen, she grins as
she tells them, "I am an INDEPENDENT WOMAN. Civiliza-
tion could shut down and I WOULD SURVIVE. When I
want a fresh chicken dinner, I simply walk out my back door
to my squawking and scattering brood. I catch one and give
it to Craig, who slits his throat quickly and mercifully with a
razor-sharp knife. We throw flowers to the wind in a memo-
rial ceremony. Then I pluck his feathers and bake him until
he's tender and golden brown. I feel proud as I eat him!"

Among a myriad of other lifestyle differences, I prefer to
buy my chicken in tidy cellophane packages at Piggly Wig-
gly. Yet I, a conservative Christian and mother of five living
on the fruited plains of Nebraska, have a deep and lasting
friendship with my liberal and "child-free" friend living in
the mountains of Oregon. I believe that my friendship with
Barbara has made an important contribution to my life and
to my children's lives. For, just as children who grow up in a
community devoid of racial diversity are likely to be uncomfortable with people from other races, so, I believe, children
who have never seen genuine love between their parents
and unbelievers are more likely to develop a superior attitude, an attitude that keeps them from building the bridges
that Christ longs for them to build.

## Friendships and our families

Barbara has some wonderful qualities: she listens to my
children, dark eyes dancing with pleasure; she remembers
them when she's traveling, sending them postcards or buy-
ing them little gifts in India or China or Guatemala; and she

gives them shoulder rubs and foot rubs, causing them to gravitate toward her like a puppy toward his master. She seems like an aunt to them, because of her love. The psalmist says that God sets the solitary in families (Psalm 68:6), and I believe He has set Barbara in our family for her benefit, and for ours. Our children know that building friendships with non-Christians can be fun, rather than a grim duty, part of our obligation because of The Great Commission.

My children have also seen obstacles in our friendship, and a genuine effort on my part (and on Barbara's) to keep those obstacles from destroying our friendship. They know, firsthand, that unfailing love is possible, even between believer and unbeliever. Solomon says, "Many a man claims to have unfailing love, but a faithful man who can find?" (Proverbs 20:6) I want my children to witness faithfulness so that they will be equipped to be faithful friends themselves.

*As my children witness faithfulness in my friendships,
they are faithful themselves. Sally and friend Tricia
in kindergarten and as seniors in high school.*

Barbara is a special gift to our family, and the bonds of our childhood are too strong for even the sword which so often divides believer from unbeliever to sever.

## The way we were

My children love Barbara, and they continually ask me to
tell them stories of when Barbara and I were little girls. The
reason my daughters particularly beg for the stories, I am
convinced, is that much about the friendships of little girls
is unchanging. The way Barbara and I were in the 1950s is
uncannily like the way little girls are with their friends today. When I tell them stories, my daughters' eyes sparkle
with identification.

Reflecting on the way Barbara and I were as children also
gives me insight into the nature of adult feminine friendship. For, though we become more sophisticated as women
and our drives are not as apparent, still, hidden in the heart
of every woman is a little girl who longs to connect.

Barbara and I grew up together, our birthdays nineteen
days apart. We cannot remember life without the other. Every summer, we were inseparable. A path running through
a woods of fragrant cedars linked our parents' Wisconsin
lakeside cottages, and countless times daily one of us was on
that path in search of the other. I would usually awaken
first, pull on my shorts, and tiptoe barefoot over the rocky
path to Barbara's cottage. I'd tap, tap, tap on her bedroom
window until her familiar grin would appear through the
glass. Then we'd be off to eat breakfast in our secret circle of
birch trees: raspberries we'd picked ourselves and Sugar
Crisp, eaten with milk in its own miniature waxpaper-lined
box. We'd swim every day, diving for rocks and floating on
our backs, soaking up the blue of the sky and the sun on our
faces — a contemplative, private, summer joy we never took
for granted. Barbara has always had a deep appreciation for
life, and I can remember her saying, as we delighted in our
mutual buoyancy, "WE ARE SO HAPPY!" And both of us,
having experienced city swimming pools teeming with hur-
tling bodies, would sigh deeply, clasp hands, and float.

There is a theory of memory that says you remember

more things when you were happy than when you were
not — and perhaps that's why my memories with Barbara
are so plentiful. We shared not only the joy of feminine
friendship, but of summer, and of childhood. All summer
long, every day, we'd play. At night, under a ceiling of stars,
we'd splash in Green Bay, cavorting like dolphins, relishing
the feel of the water gliding over our skin. Then we'd each
wrap in a blanket and lie by the crackling fire in my log cabin, sharing our hearts. If we didn't spend the night together,
one of us would be up at dawn to awaken the other for another day of summer magic.

The way Barbara and I played is the way my daughters
play today. Our games were rarely competitive; they were
relational. We blew bubbles in the sun, choreographed water ballets, and made a jewelry store on the beach with an in-
ventory of shells and seagull feathers. We'd transform
smooth oval pebbles into daisies and ladybugs with bright
enamel paint. When we talked, we connected. We'd affirm
each other's bubbles, ballets, or bright designs and delight
in the joy of connection. We told secrets and drew one another out in conversation. All this was a foreshadowing of what
was to come, for as women we are still affirmers and confiders, relishing the joy of connection.

Unlike boys our age, we were not afraid to touch each
other. We fixed each other's hair, held hands, gave each
other back rubs, and hugged when we were empathizing —
which was often!

Just as some of my most cherished childhood memories
are connected to Barbara, so are some of my most miserable.
When little girls disagree, they know where the other is vulnerable, because they have told each other their secrets.
Barbara and I would fight about the silliest things, go for
the jugular with piercing words, and separate for a long and
lonely day.

I had confided to Barbara that I was hurt that my mother

always chose to have a joint birthday party for me and my sister on August 16, which was my sister's birth date. My birthday wasn't until August 22, but by then most family and friends had left the lake to return to their homes in the city. Knowing Mom's decision made sense, yet wanting a little commiseration from Barbara, I whined, "Sometimes I feel like the party is more for my sister since it's on her real day." Barbara patted me sympathetically, agreeing that it was all quite unfair.

A week later Barbara and I were playing school — an activity Barbara tolerated and I loved. I was always the teacher and could be unbearable, as I was being that day, scolding Barbara about her misspellings. Suddenly her anger erupted.

"If you are going to be so mean, I might not come to your party." She paused to see if I would soften, but I stared sternly at her. "It really isn't *your* birthday anyhow, it's your *sister's* birthday."

"I don't care if you come," I retorted. (I cared deeply.)

Barbara shouted, "IF THAT'S TRUE, GIVE ME MY FRIENDSHIP RING BACK!"

"GLADLY!" I responded as I wrested it off my finger dramatically and threw it at her.

For the rest of the day we refused to go near the other.

Had Barbara and I not been isolated in the north woods of Wisconsin, it's likely we would have turned to other friends after one of our fights, and our friendship, like the short-lived friendships of most little girls, might have cooled and died. But we had only each other. We had to reconcile or go it alone — and little girls are not good at going it alone! Being deprived of our friendship seemed a greater deprivation than going without food or water. The next morning would find one of us giving a familiar tap on a bedroom window in lieu of an apology. Then we'd be off again, relishing the relief of reconciliation.

Because girls and women long for connection, for intimacy, we are likely to find it — but we will also find that intimacy has a Siamese twin of pain. When you are close to someone, you are devastated by transgressions, that if committed by an acquaintance would be a minor blow.

When Barbara and I were children, our unexpected arguments astonished us, like a sudden summer thunderstorm. We didn't understand that the combination of heat and our sinful natures inevitably produces such storms — nor did we have the maturity we needed to respond in such a way as to minimize the damage. And so we threw our friendship rings at each other and stomped off, like the children we were.

## And then we were women

Many adults never learn to put aside childish ways. Many women cannot maintain a lifelong friendship. Some sisters squabble until death parts them. It is vital, for our own health, and as an example to our children, to learn how to put away childish ways in our friendships and in our relationships with family members.

Barbara and I remained friends through our college years, and she was my maid of honor when I married. We stay in touch by letter and see each other, although we live 1,500 miles apart, at least every two years.

Barbara and I have surmounted differences in geography, in marital status, and in views of God. The last difference — and I'm sure Barbara would agree — has been the most difficult. Studies show that soulmate friendships usually fall apart when one has a religious conversion. Barbara and I *have* had our ups and downs — but God has answered my prayer to keep us friends despite our differences. I don't always behave maturely (though I am getting better), but God gave me the wisdom I prayed for the first time my faith in Christ caused a clash.

When my first child was born, Barbara flew to be at my

side, and I asked her to be my son's godmother. Because I was not yet a Christian, it didn't concern me when Barbara promised she would teach J.R. to worship the sun and the moon and the god within him! Asking Barbara to be J.R.'s godmother was like asking her to be my maid of honor — it was a tribute to our friendship.

A year later, however, I received Christ, and Barbara's promise came back to haunt me. More than anything else, I wanted to rear my child to know Jesus. I realized that I had to withdraw my request of Barbara to be the godmother. Would this end our friendship?

Putting myself in Barbara's shoes, I imagined she would feel hurt, maybe even betrayed. Because I feared her reaction, I put off writing the letter to tell her my decision.

One night after I had finished nursing J.R. and put him in his crib, sleepy-warm and precious in a soft bunny sleeper, I stood and watched him. His rump was in the air, his dark hair moist with sweat from the effort of nursing. He smiled as he slept, and his pacifier slipped out of his mouth. I put it gently back, and he sucked contentedly. Sweet, sweet baby. As he lay there, so innocent and vulnerable, I was overcome with motherly protection. That night I sat down to write the letter I'd been postponing. I knew that my first responsibility was to my baby — but I prayed that God would protect my friendship with Barbara. (I have come to believe since then that often we fail, as Christians, to really be sensitive to our non-Christian friends' feelings. Sometimes our motive is pride rather than a deep concern for their salvation. We speak in haste, and without love, and destroy bridges.) I believe that God, in answer to my prayer for my friendship with Barbara, gave me an extra dose of tact. I also believe He prepared Barbara's heart for what was going to be a difficult letter to read.

I wrote and revised late into the night, asking God to help me speak the truth in love. I told Barbara how I had come to trust in Jesus and how I believed His claim of being the only way to God. I told her that I wanted her involved in J.R.'s life, but that I knew we would run into conflict if she continued to be J.R.'s godmother. I told her I'd be devastated if this ended our lifelong friendship, and I pleaded with her for understanding. Finally I put the letter aside for a few days, so that I'd have more objectivity when I reread it. When I did, I sensed God's approval — so I mailed it on the wings of a prayer.

God answered my prayer: Barbara was absolutely magnanimous. She *was* hurt, but she was able to overlook her hurt in love. In fact, she was so totally forgiving that she enabled me to completely erase the whole episode from my memory. I'm not sure when I forgot, I only know that when it came up in conversation this summer, twenty-seven years later, the whole memory took me by surprise.

Barbara and I and J.R., her ex-godson, now muscled and mustached, sat on the beach together. Oblivious to our past, I began chatting insensitively about my experiences as a new godmother, a role I was holding for the first time in my life. My new goddaughter is heir to the Harley-Davidsons and I began to describe the christening reception which I'd just attended.

"Her parents have an English country home overlooking Lake Michigan in Milwaukee. They had a perfect summer day for their sumptuous garden buffet. Natalie wore a christening gown that has been in the Davidson family for three generations. . . ."

Instead of drawing me out and pressing for details, the way Barbara usually would have done, she was quiet. Then she turned to J.R. and said, "Did you know I was once your godmother?"

My first reaction was, "Could that be? Did I *really* ask *Barbara* to be J.R.'s godmother?" (And then blood rushed to my face as the memory, in detail, came back to me.) J.R.,

who is a very conservative Christian and knows Barbara
well, raised his eyebrows in disbelief. Unable to mask the
amazement in his voice, he asked, "You were?"

Barbara laughed her generous laugh. "Don't worry — I
didn't have a chance to cast my spell on you. Your mother
canceled my godmotherhood when you were still in
diapers."

I looked at Barbara to see if there was any bitterness in
her expression. There was none. I thanked God for a friend
who was able to love me even when I hurt her. And I
thanked God again for His help — which I had long
forgotten!

## Still connected

One morning this summer, shortly after sunrise, I was having my quiet time when I heard the gentle sound of a canoe
hitting the beach and turned to see my barefoot friend
climbing out, wearing a sarong from the trip she'd taken to
India with Craig. She caught my eyes, her familiar grin
brightening her suntanned face, saying, "Do you remember,
my friend, how we used to get together early in the
morning?"

I smiled back. "I remember."

This time, however, Barbara has a mug of coffee in one
hand and a cigarette in the other. And we no longer talk as
children; we discuss the mysteries of life. I ask her questions
about Jesus until she tells me she doesn't want to talk about
"religion" anymore. Tears fill my eyes at the thought that
she might not be in heaven with me but may, instead, face
the wrath of God without a Savior. I protest that this isn't
"religion" but "a relationship with Jesus Christ." Barbara
casts me a warning look and I am silenced, fearful of pushing her away from the One I want her so desperately to
know. And I ask God, in silent prayer, to show me when is
the time to speak, and when is the time to be silent. I ask

Him to show me if my desire to stay connected to Barbara is overriding His desire for me to speak. For now it seems, and I pray I am hearing Him right, that I should be silent. We walk along the beach together without words, listening to the same sounds we listened to as children: the breaking of the waves, the cries of the gulls.

Despite the fact that Barbara doesn't embrace my faith in Christ, I love her, and I am grateful to her. Barbara and I also share something that neither of us can ever again share with someone else: childhood. I feel for Barbara a special love that many women, I have discovered, feel for a sibling or a friend with whom they shared a significant part of their childhood. Though they may be vastly different as adults, their childhood memories give them a permanent place in the other's heart.

When I am reunited with Barbara, I am reminded of the girl in me. When I am with her, I feel younger, more carefree, less reserved.

I also realize that Barbara and I gave each other something else: we sharpened each other's desire and skill in nurturing. It's natural for me, as a mother, to give my children backrubs, to draw them out in conversation, and to empathize with them. In part, it's because of the way my Creator made me; and in part, it's because that's the way Barbara related to me during our formative years. I also long to have soulmates of my sex and to be a faithful friend to them. In part, that's because some of my warmest and most comforting memories are memories of my times with Barbara, and I want to repeat them in this season of my life.

**Learning to nurture**
I have come to realize, in pondering why little girls are so much closer than little boys, that one critical factor is the relationship little girls have with their mothers. By our very nature we are connected to our sex. We grow in our moth-

er's womb and nurse at her breasts. No wonder it feels so right to be connected to another female! Little boys, on the other hand, do not grow in their father's womb, but are connected to the opposite sex. When they grow up, if they have a best friend, it's usually a woman.

The mother's role is not only helpful in explaining our driving need for connectedness, but also in understanding why *some* women are *so* gifted in nurturing. If you had an especially nurturing mother, you had a head start.

This summer, as I was reflecting on the mother's role, I played Scrabble with Barbara's mother. Although I'd always known Jean to be a warm and caring woman, my research was causing me to see her with fresh appreciation. I began to realize that Jean was a big reason why Barbara was so nurturing and affirming. I was having a "Scrabble and Pie Party" for the neighbors on the shore. At my table were Jean and a sixteen-year-old friend of my daughter Sally's named Andrea. Andrea was becoming uncomfortable because her score was so much lower than either Jean's or mine. Though we tried to reassure her that it was because we'd had so many more years of Scrabble games, Andrea was unconvinced and gloomy.

The triple word score opened up and Andrea asked, "Is there such a word as quoze? I have a Q and a Z that I have had for the entire game!"

I raised my eyebrows. "Quoze?"

I was about to ask for a definition when Jean caught my eyes and said, smoothly, "Quoze. Hmmm. Could be. I wouldn't challenge it. Would you, Dee?"

I caught on. "I don't think I would."

Quoze went on the board, giving Andrea eighty-one points, and a chance to win. She brightened and began to enjoy the game. Jean and I exchanged secret smiles.

Like Barbara's mother, my own mother is a very nurturing woman, uncommonly beautiful and as feminine a woman as I've ever known. My earliest memories of her go all the way back to her lifting me from my crib. She'd cradle me against her soft and ample bosom, and brush my baby cheek with her own soft cheek, which always smelled of Pond's Cold Cream. She'd rock me and sing lullabies in her lilting soprano voice. I remember her swaying around the nursery with me, singing, "Hush little baby, don't you cry, Papa's comin home now by and by. . . ."

**In the next chapter . . .**
Women who've been blessed with a nurturing mother are likely to have rewarding friendships all of their lives. Daughters who had a cold mother or a mother who related poorly to friends herself have a harder climb ahead of them. Did you know that the proverb, "Like mother, like daughter" is from the Bible?

# Bible Study for Individuals or Small Groups

Look for commands, comparisons, and key phrases and words.
Observations are as key to accurate application for a Bible student
as measuring is to accurate cutting for a carpenter.

1 Corinthians 13:4-8

Observations:




Meaning:

Application:


1 Corinthians 13:9-12

Observations:

# And Then We Were Women

Meaning:

Application:

1 Peter 3:13-17

Observations:

Meaning:

Application:

Psalm 68:4-6

Observations:

Meaning:

Application:

*By the time Caroline was a year
and a half old ... we had an elaborate
lovers' ritual to follow. When she was ready
for bed, in double diapers and pajamas,
I'd ask her: Do you want some
mama nursee? She'd nod or say yes and ...
literally run, to the rocking chair. ...
Within two minutes total contentment would
absorb her and those blue-gray eyes
would close. Calling it a lovers' ritual is not
an exaggeration: I was her first love, and
the depth and completeness of my response to her
taught her about the possibilities
of love for the rest of her life.*

Connie Marshner, *Can Motherhood Survive?*[1]

three
# Never Underestimate the Power of a Mother

Mail has come to me in a steady stream since the release of *The Friendships of Women.* As a result of these often heart-wrenching letters, I have come to see how influential our relationship with our mothers is in shaping the way we relate to others, particularly to women, for the rest of our lives. For example, a common response to a cold mother is longing for a woman to love you, sometimes to the precipice of homosexuality, as this letter demonstrates:

> My mother stopped showing me affection when I reached the age of five, telling me I was "too old for that." . . . I always wished that I could stay a little girl, so that I wouldn't lose her love. Today, as a woman, I have no interest in guys, marriage, or sex—just a desperate yearning to be loved, to be embraced, to be cherished—by an older woman.

Another response to a cold or harsh mother is to pull away from women, to be wary of being hurt again, as this letter shows:

> A few years ago, in an attempt to bring some healing to my relationship with my mother, I opened up to her, telling her how much I needed her. She hasn't spoken to me since. I didn't realize, until I heard you speak at our retreat in Florida, that this is why I mistrust women, don't have any close women friends, and have been promiscuous with men in a crazy attempt to meet my needs for intimacy.

On the other side, a mother who is loving and nurturing toward her daughter is preparing her for love for the rest of her life.

Carol Kent, the author of *The Secret Longings of the Heart* (NavPress) is one of the most nurturing women I've ever met. I interviewed Carol when she was giving a retreat at our church. She came to my home after speaking, slipped off her heels, put her feet up, and opened up to me as if she'd known me all her life. Carol's childhood home sounded like a chapter from *Little Women,* with five close and loving sisters. Carol's stories led me to call one of those sisters: Jennie Dimkoff. Again, I found myself talking to an incredibly warm and nurturing woman. Carol and Jennie are affirmers, confiders, hostesses in conversation — the kind of women you want for best friends. Being with them is like snuggling up to a roaring fire in a ski lodge with a mug of hot chocolate — warmth goes down to the center of your being and you feel renewed, ready to go out and face the cold again. It didn't surprise me to find out that their mother was this kind of woman as well.

## Mother love

Jennie shared with me how, when she and her husband moved from Michigan to Louisiana, she missed her mother and was sometimes haunted by the times she knew she had hurt her mom during her teenage years.

"Feeling homesick, I called Mom and told her how much I missed her — but I never mentioned my other concern. Then one day while we were back in Michigan visiting, I came in the back door, and there she was, asleep in the living room rocker. I stood there and watched her, my heart so full of love for her. I thought of the years she had prayed for and nurtured me and been there for me as well as for my five siblings. I knelt on the floor and laid my head in her lap. She woke and stroked my hair like I was a little girl again. That day I asked her to forgive me for all the times I had made her cry when I was a teenager. Her response was: 'Oh Jennie, I love you, and I forgave you so long ago.' Her response to me that day was as nurturing to me as an adult, as any tenderness she showed me in my childhood."

Jennie gave me some wonderful insights into the rippling power of mother love by sharing with me a talk she gives on Jochebed, the mother of Miriam, Aaron, and Moses. If you grew up in a Bible-preaching church, you probably heard the story of baby Moses in the bulrushes more times than you care to remember — but stay with me, because I have a fresh insight for you.

Pharaoh had ordered that all Jewish males be murdered

the instant they were delivered. Did Jochebed's hopes soar when she heard that the Hebrew midwives were disobeying the Pharaoh and allowing the baby boys to live? And did they plummet when she was told of Pharaoh's Plan B: to have his troops come in, seek out the baby boys, and throw them in the Nile?

I, like many women, was prone to wild dreams when I was pregnant. Solomon tells us that we dream about what we worry about! (Ecclesiastes 5:3) If I had been Jochebed, nightmares of screaming babies, swords, and crocodiles would have kept me tossing and turning.

When Moses was born, Jochebed developed an elaborate plan to save him — and her daughter Miriam played a key role. How this drama must have shaped Miriam! If you are an older sister, your mother probably coached you in nurturing your younger siblings, but for Jochebed and Miriam the stakes were life or death. I can picture Miriam hiding with Moses in the closet, honey on her thumb, praying he wouldn't cry when the soldiers prowled past their home. Miriam probably helped Jochebed coat the papyrus basket with tar and pitch, praying with her mother as they worked. And I'm sure Jochebed role played with Miriam how to respond if the princess found Moses. Jennie Dimkoff imagines Jochebed's parting before she leaves Miriam and Moses at the river:

> She holds Moses one last time, feeling the velvet softness of his face in her neck, and her heart hurts. She puts him in the basket and covers him carefully. She hitches up her skirt in her waistband, picks up that basket on her hip, and steps into the reeds while Miriam, with pounding heart, watches. Then Jochebed comes back on shore and faces a little girl, saying: "Remember everything we practiced honey . . . I love you so — Oh, don't be afraid Miriam — God is with you." . . . And then she does the hardest thing in her life. She walks away from her two vulnerable children and leaves them in God's hands.[2]

I have little doubt that one of the reasons that Miriam grew up to be the first woman prophet and a leader of literally millions of women was that she had a mother like Jochebed. Jochebed, because she was determined to choose life for Moses, taught Miriam crucial skills in nurturing, skills that would open up possibilities of love to her for the rest of her life.

## The rippling impact of choosing life or death

One of the reasons abortion rates have soared is that we tend to repeat the sins of our mothers. If a woman who has had an abortion doesn't experience the forgiveness that's possible through Christ, she'll have to find another way to live with the blood on her hands. Many become intensely pro-choice, trying futilely to justify their sin. Their hearts harden, their nurturing tendencies wither. If their own daughters become pregnant at a difficult time, they are likely to counsel them to take their child's life. The sins of the mothers, like the sins of the fathers, can be passed on from generation to generation. The proverb, "Like mother, like daughter," is actually used in a negative sense in Ezekiel 16:44.

I have a dear friend who works in a Crisis Pregnancy Center. Repeatedly she has had the experience of counseling a young girl who wants to carry her baby to term, but is facing enormous pressure from parents or a boyfriend. When my friend called one sixteen-year-old who had had a positive pregnancy test, the girl wept and explained, "Mom is taking me to Kansas City in the morning for an abortion. [Tears] No, you can't talk to her, because she's already asleep. We have to leave at five in the morning. She wouldn't listen anyhow — she says there's nothing to talk about."

This girl's position is not unusual. *Ladies Home Journal* asked their readers if they would "encourage" their teenage daughters to have an abortion, and found that thirty-one percent would.[3] While I believe many of these mothers are well-meaning, I am convinced that the negative impact of pushing your daughter to take her baby's life multiplies in destruction down through the generations.

However, the reverse is true: if we had a mother like Jochebed, who valued life, and taught her daughter to trust God and to protect life, no matter how difficult the circumstances, we are likely to instill the same values in our daughters.

Lee Ezell tells a captivating story in her book, *The Missing Piece*. Lee lost her virginity to a rapist when she was a teenager. During that rape she conceived the only child she would ever carry in her womb. Because Lee feared and loved God, she decided against abortion and visited an adoption agency. The social worker at that agency carried herself "with a military bearing" and thrust a computerized form into Lee's hands so she could help choose her baby's adoptive parents. The form gave Lee a choice of Protestant, Catholic, Jewish, or none. Lee spoke up, asking the social worker to write down that she wanted her baby placed in a Bible-believing home.

The authoritarian woman glared at Lee, and said, "There ain't no box like that, girl. You got your choices. Now don't give me a hard time." When Lee persisted, the social worker slammed her case file shut. "We'll talk about this next time."[4] Then she mumbled under her breath and gave Lee a card for another appointment.

Before she returned, Lee read over the story of Moses and was strengthened by Jochebed's example. Reflectively, Lee writes, "Jochebed did not abandon her child to fate. She did not cave in to Pharaoh's awesome power. She did not let the potential criticism of other women determine her course of action."[5]

When Lee returned to the adoption agency, the social worker stared at her and said, "Now, are you going to give me any problems today?"

With her biggest smile, Lee answered, "Not as long as the line about my child going into a Bible-believing home stays on the application."

The line stayed. And just as God had a plan for Moses, He had a plan for Lee's baby, Julie. Julie grew up in a wonderful home with parents who truly loved the Lord.

And Julie, as an adult, a beautiful young woman who looks almost identical to her mother Lee, was involved with the pro-life movement even before she knew she'd been conceived through rape. In the book, *What My Parents Did Right,* Julie Makimaa shares how that news impacted her: "I began to speak out against abortion, sharing my convictions — which were now stronger than ever — that *every* pre-born child deserves the right to live. . . . I was a prophet called to speak out for the pre-born who had been conceived under circumstances similar to mine."[6]

*Lee & Julie*

## Withdrawal

Experts say that our basic sense of feeling connected or separated from others is rooted in our experience as infants with our mothers. The two most common responses to having a mother who lacks "mother love" are withdrawal and dependency.

Withdrawal is the natural response to pain. In Foster Cline's paper, "Understanding and Treating the Severely Disturbed Child," he writes, "It's as if a voice inside their heads is saying, 'I trusted you to be there and to take care of me, and you weren't. It hurts so much that I will not trust anyone, ever. I must control everything—and everybody—to ward off being abandoned again.' "[7]

When we adopted our daughter Annie from an overseas orphanage at the age of five, she was wary and withdrawn. For economic reasons, her mother had to relinquish her. To Anne's memory, after she had been taken to the orphanage, no one cradled her in their arms to ease her pain. Instead, she was perched on a stool and her lovely long hair was shorn. There were hundreds of babies and children, but only a few caretakers with frayed nerves. There wasn't time for stories or hugs! Anne remembers being awakened rudely each morning by a woman who would jostle her and yell: "Get up and help with the babies!"

Anne was not able to tell me about all this for a few months, as she didn't speak English. But I knew the moment I laid eyes on her that she was hurting. It took time and patience to break through Anne's shell, and sometimes I would find myself becoming angry at her lack of response. She became quite ill during her first week with us. When I would pull her on my lap and rock her, she would stiffen. When I would try to coax a smile from her with nursery rhymes or peek-a-boo, she would scowl at me. When I gave her cough syrup, she would spit it back out at me. There were times when I wanted to shake her.

Waiting for Anne to open up and flower seemed to take forever. Just when my patience was growing the thinnest, God provided a six-year-old to model long-suffering for me.

Sarena Luke had been praying for Anne, nightly, ever since she'd learned, six months earlier, that we would be adopting a little girl. I will never forget the day they met face-to-face.

We stopped at Sarena's home, where Sarena ran down the steps eagerly, pigtails flying, to greet Anne. She had a teddy bear, which she placed in Anne's hands.

Anne took that teddy bear and threw it down on the ground.

Resiliently, Sarena reached out for Anne's hand, saying, "Anne, let's go swing." Anne jerked her hand away.

Sarena pled with Anne. "Anne, I just want to be your friend."

Anne didn't understand English, and she scowled at Sarena.

*Annie & Sarena*

I will never forget Sarena's response. She looked at me and said, "Mrs. Brestin, I don't care how long it takes. I'm going to just keep on being nice to Anne, and one day we're going to be best friends."

God used Sarena, along with others, to restore Anne.

Anne has discovered that she can trust others. But it took time and the kind of love that doesn't give up, like that of the Lord!

Some girls, deprived of a caring mother, never have a Christlike friend or a mother figure in their lives. If they don't grow up to be withdrawn, they are likely to go the other way, and cling to their friends with emotional desperation.

## Dependence

I've received countless letters in response to the story I told in *The Friendships of Women* of the woman I called Rachel, whom God is continuing to deliver from the bondage of homosexuality. The reasons for falling into homosexuality are varied, but one common contributing factor, according to Dr. Salle de-Garmo, who runs a Christian Counseling Center for Women in Denver, is growing up with a withdrawn mother. My friend Rachel also believes, though this is controversial, that, because of the Fall, there may be a contributing genetic tendency, just as for some alcoholics there is a contributing genetic tendency.

But Rachel shares, with real hope, "You wouldn't tell an alcoholic who has a contributing genetic tendency or who has had a dysfunctional childhood that there is no hope for him! Not at all! We've seen millions delivered through the power of God. It's so unfair to take away their hope, telling them that is the way they are and must always be. So it is with a woman trapped in a lesbian relationship. She will have to make some hard choices, but God can provide a way and bless her with a fulfilling life of healthy relationships. She *will* have to separate emotionally and physically from the woman she has fallen with, and she *will* have to get help, and she *will* have to repeatedly offer up her desires to the Lord, BUT SHE CAN BE ASSURED THAT GOD WILL CONTINUE TO DELIVER HER AS SHE ACTS IN OBE-

DIENCE! In time, I was able to have a friendship with the woman I had fallen with—but we had to wait until both of our motives were defined and pure. We are living proof of the power of Christ and so are many many other women who were once trapped in the bondage of lesbianism. We know we will always be vulnerable to this sin, just as alcoholics consider themselves vulnerable to alcohol, but we also know the victory of continual deliverance!"

Rachel and I have both referred women struggling with homosexuality to Exodus International. Some of the ways they can help are through seminars, counseling, literature, and tapes. They have about seventy agencies in the U.S. and also an overseas network. Their address is Exodus, P.O. Box 2121, San Rafael, CA 94912 (415/454–1017).

Married women struggling with homosexuality often wish to keep this a secret from their husbands. Knowing how important honesty is in a marriage, I asked Rachel about this dilemma. She said, "If your marriage is not stable, and it is possible to separate from this friendship physically and to draw back emotionally without telling your husband, then you can begin that way. But if you cannot separate or get help without telling him, then you must tell him, or your marriage is doomed anyhow."

Most women who struggle with dependency do not cross the line into physical intimacy, but envelop their friends, driving them away with their neediness.

When we lived in Akron, I met Shannon, whom I liked very much. But before long, I began to crave space. She wanted to see me or talk at length on the phone every day. If I told her what a busy day I was having, or that I needed time with my family, I sensed her pain. I didn't want to hurt her, but I was having trouble coping with the demands she was making on me as a friend. Proverbs 25:17 says, "Seldom set foot in your neighbor's house—too much of you, and he will hate you."

That was the way I was beginning to feel when I heard the phone or the doorbell. Though I'm not proud to admit this, there were times when I didn't answer, but instead held my breath and didn't move, hoping desperately she would give up and go away. One time when I saw Shannon coming up the walk, I scooped the boys into a closet and hushed them. Five-year-old J.R. said, loudly, "Mommy, isn't this like telling a lie?"

If I had known then what I know now, I think I would have been a wiser friend with Shannon. Shannon was just three when her mother had abandoned her and her father, never to return. What Shannon needed, as an adult, was Christian counseling and a friend who would put some boundaries on the friendship. God might have used me to bring healing to Shannon. Instead, I fled — wounding her again.

It is intriguing to me that often God does bring a mother figure into a hurting woman's life, and, in so doing, helps her to break the chain in Christ.

## Breaking the chain

I found Lee Ezell's story in Gloria Gaither's book, *What My Parents Did Right.* When I saw Lee's name in the table of contents, I thought, "I'm not surprised Lee had a nurturing mother — that's why she was able to make the hard choice of life for the daughter conceived by rape." But when I read Lee's story it was in a section entitled "Breaking the Cycle." Lee didn't have nurturing parents! Instead, her father was a violent alcoholic and her mother, to protect herself, built an impenetrable armor around herself, keeping out not only her husband, but, unfortunately, her five children as well. Lee says, "In my home, there was never any expression of caring or love; I knew only defensive survival tactics."[8]

Lee came to Christ through a Billy Graham Crusade, but she is quick to tell you that that didn't heal all of her childhood wounds. Key to Lee's recovery, she is convinced, was forgiveness. "Only when we are able to forgive can the doors to emotional wholeness swing open and the healing process begin."[9]

I heard this same thought echoed by Carolyn Koons. Carolyn and I were co-speakers at a retreat in Gull Lake, Michigan. Carolyn is the author of *Beyond Betrayal,* the story of her recovery from a childhood of abuse. Carolyn's father, like Lee's, was a violent alcoholic. His violence resulted in the death of Carolyn's baby brother — an event etched in Carolyn's memory. On another horrible day, Carolyn's mother held a gun to Carolyn's head, telling her that her father hated her and would one day kill her. How do you overcome having a mother like that?

Carolyn told me she was slow to trust women, feeling that they too would betray her. But in Christ she is now a whole and loving woman with many healthy friendships. After she spoke, women lined up to talk to her — women, who, like her, had missed having a loving and nurturing mother. Carolyn, like Lee, says the road to recovery is not a short one — and counseling is surely advisable. Carolyn shared a list of helpful books with those who came to her, a few of which I have listed in the notes to this chapter.[10]

Both of these women were able to break the cycle, becoming loving mothers themselves and providing hope for those with similar backgrounds. It is intriguing to me that in both of these women's cases God provided a "mother figure," a godly and nurturing woman who befriended them and held out a lifeline. In Lee's case it was "Mom Croft," who provided a shelter for Lee in her home during Lee's pregnancy. In Carolyn's case, when she was a teenager living on her own in a trailer, she got a phone call from a woman named Jean Fonner who invited her to church. Carolyn cussed her out, but Jean kept calling, kept visiting, kept on until she loved Carolyn into the kingdom.

Mom Croft and Jean Fonner show us the difference we can make in the lives of women who've been deprived of a caring and nurturing mother. By reaching out to those who didn't have the advantage we did, we can help make a difference, not only in their lives, but in the lives of generations to come.

**In the next chapter . . .**
Seeing the power of the mother/daughter connection has given me understanding into the intensity of little girls' friendships. If you want to help the girls in your life form healthy friendships, you need to understand this intense desire for connection.

Come with me into the charming, yet sometimes treacherous, world of girls.

# Bible Study for Individuals or Small Groups

Read the historical account, putting yourself in the place of the people involved in order to observe more. Observe adjectives and adverbs to help get into their skin. An example of making observations on a narrative passage is given in the Bible study notes at the end of the book.

Exodus 1:8-22

Observations:

Principles to apply:

Application:

# And Then We Were Women

Exodus 2:1-10

Observations:




Principles to apply:

Application:

Exodus 15:19-21

Observations:




Principles to apply:

Application:

*"We must join hands—so," said Anne gravely.*
*"It ought to be over running water.*
*We'll just imagine this path is running water.*
*I'll repeat the oath first. I solemnly swear*
*to be faithful to my bosom friend, Diana Barry,*
*as long as the sun and moon shall endure.*
*Now you say it and put my name in."*

L.M. Montgomery, *Anne of Green Gables*[1]

four

# Understanding the Girls in Your Life

We recently returned from our summer place in Ephraim, Wisconsin. We were blessed to be reunited there with extended family, who vacation in cottages nestled in the woods lining Green Bay. Two summers ago Anne was introduced to her third cousin, Lani. Since Anne is adopted, she and Lani are not related by blood, but they have decided otherwise. Lani has lovely olive skin, darkened by living year-round in Maui. Her hair is long and straight and dark, like Anne's. Her coloring is the closest Anne has seen to her own Korean coloring since she moved from Seoul to our racially impoverished land of central Nebraska. When Anne and Lani met they stole shy glances at each other, vainly trying to swallow the smiles welling up from deep within — smiles born of the joy of connecting. Within an hour they were whispering, conspiring, sharing secrets. They spent hours choreographing a dance to Amy Grant's song, "Every Heartbeat." When they dance, they hold hands, swirl around each other, sway in synchronization, and beam at each other, flashing smiles with missing teeth. As is characteristic of females of every age, they face each other when they sit. (In contrast, males sit side-by-side.) One evening I looked out our window to see Anne and Lani seated on the dock. Though the sunset was spectacular, they were not facing it, they were facing each other, sitting Indian-style, knees touching. Silhouetted by the sun sinking into Green Bay, their small figures made a triangle, heads touching. They call each other "Cousin" and their connection satisfies the relentless hunger females have for intimacy.

### The way they play

The uppermost desire for most girls in their play is connection. Therefore they will abandon a game that is causing conflict. The uppermost desire for boys, in contrast, is to establish status. They often take turns showing off for each other, on their bikes or on playground equipment. Boys are more comfortable with competitive games and less troubled by conflict. Recently I watched Anne and her friend Geri abandon a Monopoly game rather than continue their conflict over when you can buy houses. Connection was more important than winning. They packed it away in good humor and began practicing their cartwheels.

*So true of me*

A study of preschoolers by Jacqueline Sachs found that little girls were much more cooperative when they played than were little boys. When they were playing doctor and baby, the boys wanted to take the doctor role 79 percent of the time, and would often get into long arguments about which boy would get this high-status role. The girls, on the other hand, would ask each other what role they wanted ("Will you be the patient for a few minutes?") or made a joint proposal ("I'll be the nurse and you be the doctor"; "Now we can both be doctors"; "We both can be sick"; or "Okay, and I'll be the doctor for my baby and you be the doctor for your baby").[2]

Girls' play is characterized by symmetry. Our home has a bathroom with double sinks. Countless times I have peeked in to see Annie bathing a Cabbage Patch doll in one sink while her friend is bathing a Cabbage Patch doll in the other. And they are making plans for continued symmetry. ("When we are done, we will dress them, fix their hair, and take them to backyard Bible club where we will sing.")

One of my favorite book series when I was a little girl was Sydney Taylor's *All-of-a-kind-Family*. (These are great books to read to your daughters in order to encourage sister love!) In her books, five Jewish sisters show the kind of symmetrical play that is typical of little girls. In the following incident, the sisters have hidden bags of penny candy under their pillows.

> The room was in darkness save for the gas light which shone from the kitchen through the opened bedroom door. Lucky for them! One look at their guilty faces, and Mama would have known that something was up. But Mama suspected nothing. . . . Tucking in the featherbed, Mama said goodnight to all and went out, shutting the bedroom door behind her.
>
> The fun could begin at last! Charlotte directed because the game was hers.

> "First we take a chocolate baby, and we eat only the head." They bit off the heads and chewed away contentedly. . . .[3]

Not only do little girls play differently than little boys, they talk differently.

## The way they talk

In her book, *You Just Don't Understand: Men and Women in Conversation,* sociolinguist Deborah Tannen says, "For girls, talk is the glue that holds relationships together. Boys' relationships are held together primarily by activities."[4]

Tannen described an experiment in which pairs of second graders, boys and girls, were put in a professor's room before a videocamera on a tripod and instructed to "talk about something serious."

Kevin and Jimmy found the assignment too foreign — unable to accomplish it, they squirmed and made faces, jumped out of their chairs, made motor sounds by trilling their lips and uttering nonsense syllables, and took turns mugging before the camera. They bemoaned the fact that they weren't outside playing football and made plans to ride bikes together soon.

The assignment was much easier for Ellen and Jane, for serious conversation is characteristic of the friendships of girls. When the professor left the room, they huddled together, pulling their chairs close, and began to converse — not in short spurts of speech, like the boys, but in long blocks of matching stories. Obeying the professor's instructions to talk about something serious very literally, they each searched their memories for accidents or mishaps. Ellen told of how her uncle had fallen off a ladder. Jane then told of an uncle who had been gored by a bull. Rewarding her friend for succeeding with the assignment, Ellen said, "That's serious."[5]

The matching of experiences is a way to bond. It's a way of saying, "We are alike." When girls are little, their matching of experiences is quite simple. They simply go back and forth, as Ellen and Jane did when they each shared about an uncle who had a serious injury. One shares a story, and then the other will connect by saying, "I know," and then shares her matching story. As girls mature, their matching of experiences forms a more intricate web. They may still connect with, "I know," but they are more likely to draw one another out about their thoughts, to affirm, and to empathize. Instead of simply taking turns sharing experiences, they create a stronger bonding experience. The following is a conversation which I overheard between our daughter Sally and her friend Helen Reeve, who is in her twenties:

> SALLY: I'm reading Frank Peretti's *This Present Darkness.*
>
> HELEN: I read that too! Isn't it great?
>
> SALLY: It is. But I'm not going to read it at night anymore. I get too scared.
>
> HELEN: I know. When I tried that I had to check under the bed!
>
> SALLY: Did you really? I'm so glad — because I was feeling silly. After I finally stopped reading and turned the light off last night, I heard noises everywhere. I lay there for hours — ready to jump out of my skin.
>
> HELEN: (laughs and puts her arm comfortingly around Sally) Oh, poor Sally! I understand exactly!

Girls, much more frequently than boys, tie up the phone, write long notes to each other in school, and confide the most intimate of secrets to each other. Girls commiserate much more than boys, because commiserating reaps the reward of connecting. Louisa May Alcott captures this in her opening of *Little Women:*

> "Christmas won't be Christmas without any presents," grumbled Jo, lying on the rug.
>
> "It's so dreadful to be poor!" sighed Meg, looking down at her old dress.
>
> "I don't think it's fair for some girls to have plenty of pretty things, and other girls nothing at all," added little Amy, with an injured sniff.[6]

It's fascinating to read the Song of Songs through the perspective of teenage girls' friendships. The Shulammite maiden was very likely a teenager, and she and her girlhood friends talk excitedly about her romance, her wedding, and her love life with Solomon. The groom's friends are not part of the story at all. The Shulammite maiden seems to be his only source of intimacy, his only confidante. Though she is obviously close to Solomon, she still needs her young friends. She runs to them when she and Solomon have their first quarrel (Song of Songs 5:2–6:1). She continually confides in them – not only when she's sad, but when she's happy.

Young women are enthralled with romance because romance satisfies their strong drive for connection. They find vicarious pleasure in hearing the details of each other's romances. When teenage boys talk to each other, their conversation reflects instead their drive for status, talking about cars, sports, or topping one another with jokes. Many wouldn't be caught dead admitting to romantic feelings – but would eagerly brag about their sexual conquests (real or imagined).

An example of this occurs in the movie *Grease,* a story about teenagers in the '50s. Danny gives a musical rendition of "locker room" talk. His friends ask him about his summer romance with Sandy and he highly exaggerates their sexual activity in order to impress his friends and establish status. His longing with his friends is not so much for connection, but for status. He also doesn't want to admit that he cares for Sandy romantically because that might mean a loss of status in his friends' eyes. Real men (they think!) stay independent.

The camera then turns to Sandy, where she begins with "He was really romantic . . ." and the girls respond with rapturous smiles of identification. Then we hear the truth about the sexual relationship (It was very innocent — they strolled, held hands, drank lemonade . . . )! Sandy's longing with her friends is not so much to establish status, but to connect. She knows that they will empathize with the joy of romantic connection, and she fills them in on all the dreamy details, and, in so doing, connects with them and provides them with vicarious pleasure.

### The way they influence

Boys' groups are often formed on the basis of interests rather than popularity. In our junior high, three of the groups are "The Skaters" (boys who have skateboards and long hair), "The Jocks," and "The Brains." In each of these

*Illustration A: Boys*

groups, the boy with the highest status has achieved different accomplishments. If you belong to "The Skaters," you want to excel in skateboarding, holding your liquor, and scoring with girls — because that is what the boy with the highest status has accomplished. It is interesting that there are many warnings in Proverbs to boys about not running with the rebellious bunch. (See Proverbs 1:10-19.) The diagram on page 65 illustrates the hierarchical structure which is typical of boys' groups:

One of the most helpful things we can do for our sons is to pray and guide them toward groups where the boy with the highest status is likely to be respected for his godliness rather than his ungodliness. In choosing churches, we've looked for strong youth programs and godly male leadership. And we've hosted the para-church ministries in our homes (such as Fellowship of Christian Athletes and Youth for Christ) in hopes of encouraging our sons to become active in those kinds of groups. We've also extended hospitality to godly young men whom our boys have admired — because mentors, rather than best friends, hold enormous influence. Often, after dinner or a time of shooting baskets, our boys have listened to them and soaked in their godly standards. Boys want to be like males who have status in their eyes.

This approach is good with daughters as well, but the friend who has the most influence on a girl is not necessarily the most popular girl, or the girl with the highest status. She does have influence, but not to the degree that the best friend does. Girls, who long to stay connected, do not want to risk separation from their best friends. Therefore, it is possible that a girl may be making different choices than the girl with the highest status, if her best friend is as well. Girls groups are structured more like a spiral than a hierarchy, as the diagram on page 67 illustrates:

Because talk, rather than activities, is the glue that holds girls' friendships together, girls have more power to influence each other's thoughts and values. The Song of Songs illustrates this beautifully.

*Illustration B: Girls*

The Shulammite maiden is close to her friends. Repeatedly she warns them, "Daughters of Jerusalem, I charge you: Do not arouse or awaken love until it so desires" (Song of Songs 2:7, 3:5, 8:4). She is saying in effect, "Sexual passion is so powerful! It's difficult to stop once it's awakened! Therefore, don't arouse it. Don't lift the lid of intimacy even slightly until you are married!" She is thankful that she didn't, and encourages her friends to guard their hearts as well.

We go to a Bible-preaching church, but I would be naive if I assumed that everyone who attended was strong in the Lord. I have observed that unless at least the mother is living a transformed life and has grasped the vision of discipling her children, the children are not likely to be strong enough to withstand the tides of the world when they hit their teens.

When our daughter Sally was in fifth grade, I had a coffee for about six mothers of fifth-grade girls in our city. They represented four different churches and had in common a vision for discipling their daughters. In two years our daughters would all be in the same junior high. I told the mothers I'd gathered them together hoping that we could come up with some plans which would encourage friendships between our daughters. Then they'd be better equipped to help each other face the pressure ahead. We spent the morning praying and brainstorming. Three particular plans resulted that were pivotal in our daughters' lives.

Four of us with girls in the same elementary school decided that during the sex education day (during which information which was contrary to our standards of morality was dispensed) we'd keep our girls home and have them get together for games, discussion, and prayer. That was much easier for them than sitting alone in a study hall (the school's awkward plan for opting out). It also helped them to identify one another.

We invited our daughters to a weekly Bible study for the fifty days before Easter each year. (We were inspired by the radio program, "The Chapel of the Air," which provides materials for a "50 Day Adventure" for varying age groups.) We took turns hosting the girls for donuts before school. We did this each year for fifth, sixth, and seventh grades.

When our girls were in high school, one family hosted a weekly before-school prayer time for parents and their kids.

Eight years after our first meeting, when our daughters were seniors in high school, each mother had seen fruit. From my vantage point, as Sally's mother, here is some that God has allowed me to see:

• Sally, Robyn, and Dionne often discern that a teacher is coming from a Godless viewpoint. They have secret signals to one another to be alert, to guard their hearts!

- Sally, Shun-Yenn, Dionne, Robyn, and Jordan have decided that they will date only strong Christians.
- Sally and Shun-Yenn attended a two-week academic camp together in Colorado for Christian leadership called Summit Ministries. This not only helped them discern the secular mind-set of the public school, but convinced them both that if they married, they only wanted to marry a spiritual giant — because they saw the difference in guys!
- Jordan, Andrea, and Shun-Yenn are long-distance friends now that they've moved away to three different states. But they stay in touch with the others by letter, encouraging one another to be true to the Lord. All have come back to visit. One summer Andrea came to Wisconsin to vacation with us for ten days. When she arrived, she was carrying Elisabeth Elliot's book, *Passion and Purity.* Sally said, "I'm reading that too! We can read together!" Then Andrea showed Sally her "Promise Ring," which her father had given her in exchange for her promise to remain pure until she married. Sally thrust out her hand and said, "I know! My dad did the same thing with me! See?" (And her sister Anne, the domino next in line, was soaking it all in.)
- Sally, Dionne, Robyn, Julie, and Holly have teamed together for Christian ministry: visiting nursing homes, teaching Sunday School, and reaching out to their class evangelistically through Fellowship of Christian Athletes. At Robyn's surprise seventeenth birthday party, Sally and Dionne led the other fifteen girls in a time of prayer for their senior class.
- Sally, Dionne, and Robyn don't go to the regular school dances because "the couples are enmeshed, the music is raunchy, and drinking often follows." Sally and Dionne have gone to Prom and Homecoming, but they have tactfully explained to their dates that they want to go just as friends — and don't want to be enmeshed when dancing. The boys, who have been Christians, have been supportive!

I'm so thankful that when we met as mothers, years ago, the Lord was with us. To be honest, we didn't always see eye-to-eye. When mothers talk about the "correct" way to raise children, they can become like mother bears. At one point a disagreement was so sharp we separated and formed two different groups for our 50-Day Adventure. But God enabled us to reconcile, work together again, and reach our destination.

In hindsight, I know I gained by being with mothers who were much stricter than I — and I think they may have gained from being with those of us who were more permissive. (In fact, Shell and I started lovingly calling each other "Law" and "Grace" and believe that God gave us our friendship, in part, to bring us each more toward the middle.) Christian women should be able to put away childish ways and work together for a common purpose. If we could do that, not only would we accomplish more, but we could better model for our daughters godly ways to deal with conflict in female friendships.

### Showing our daughters level paths

Hebrews 12:13 says: "Make level paths for your feet, so that the lame may not be disabled, but rather healed." Childhood is the time we have to help our children discover level paths. If we don't, they may become permanently disabled in relating to others. I do not agree with those who feel they should stay out of their childrens' squabbles — whether they be with siblings or with friends. These are the formative years! As mothers, or as mentors, God gives us opportunities to help girls learn how to relate to their friends in a healthy way, and, in so doing, help them form habits that will enhance their relationships their whole lives long. And when girls are hurting because of friendship pain, they're teachable, like fallow ground ready to receive good seed!

I often look for a Scripture to help my daughter know how

to respond to someone who is being unkind. When Sally was a freshman in high school, she experienced friction with a sophomore girl, whom I'll call Sue. Whenever their paths crossed, the sophomore girl rolled her eyes and whispered and giggled with her friends.

Sally and I prayed about it and the Scripture that came to mind was "Do not be overcome by evil, but overcome evil with good" (Romans 12:21). Sally and I role played different ways she could apply this verse with Sue. Sally pretended to be Sue and showed me how she glared whenever Sally walked past her table in art. Taking Sally's part, I smiled and said, "Hi, Sue! I saw your tennis scores in the paper. They were great!"

Sally said, "Oh, Mom, I don't know if I can do that. She'll just glare at me."

I said, "Probably! But Proverbs [25:15] tells us that "a gentle tongue can break hard bones." If you are persistently warm and friendly, I think Sue's hardness will break. I'm excited, Sally, to see what God is going to do!"

Sally flew into the house after school the next day and said, "I did it! Sue looked stunned!" And after school I saw her and — you will not believe this, Mom — Sue said, 'Hi!' "

Of course, our plans have not always produced the desired result, and if my child seems to be banging her head against the wall, I suggest that she lay that friendship down for a time and seek other friends. It's important that she leave the door open and remain friendly, but it's very possible the friendship needs a rest. Sometimes enthusiastic young gardeners can overwater, overwork — and the plants would do better if left alone for a while.

Some girls are more successful in friendship than are others — and often those girls have a mother or a godly older woman who mentored and guided them. Likewise, some sisters are close growing up, and some turn their home into a battleground.

## In the next chapter . . .

The sister relationship has parallels to friendship, but additional dynamics are at work. For example, many older sisters can remember exercising their power over a younger sister. Tania Aebi, who is fourteen months older than her sister Nina, reminisced how she and her best friend, "in a fit of adolescent cruelty," tricked Nina:

> We gouged out the chocolate chips in some cookies, replaced them carefully with small, black rabbit droppings and offered them to Nina. . . . Before asking why I was being so uncharacteristically nice, she popped one in her mouth. We then told her what she was eating and doubled over in laughter.[7]

Why is it that big sisters can be so mean and little sisters such brats?

# Bible Study for Individuals or Small Groups

Read the historical account, putting yourself in the place of the people involved in order to observe more. Ask *Who? What? Why? How?*

Song of Songs 2:7 (It's repeated in 3:5 and 8:4, so look at those contexts as well.)

Observations:

Principles to apply:

Application:

## And Then We Were Women

Song of Songs 5:2–6:1

Observations:

Principles to apply:

Application:

Song of Songs 8:8-10 (Note that this is a flashback to the Shulammite's family home.)

Observations:

Principles to apply:

Application:

*Incident remembered by
Carol Kent, the eldest of five
sisters and a brother.*

## five
# Such Devoted Sisters

Being the eldest sister can be hard work! As Carol Kent said, in commenting on the incident in the above cartoon, "I was the one in charge, but I had absolutely no control. They were naughty children. It was hard work. And I wasn't being paid for it. This is the job of the older sister."

When our first grandchild, Emily Jae Brestin, was born,

our son John and daughter-in-law Julie were delighted to have a girl because they hoped (at that point) to have a quiver full (five) of children and they knew a girl would probably be more help with younger siblings. When they told me this, we were seated in the hospital room and I was cradling my beautiful granddaughter, tiny and pink, a fragile rosebud. My mind flashed back to Carol's story, and I thought, "Here it begins. Here it starts. Poor little Emmie! So much work ahead of you!"

Older sisters tend to work harder, but they have also been known to abuse their age advantage. Elizabeth Fishel, author of *Sisters,* explains that "dominating younger siblings gives older siblings an illusion of power in an unfree world."[1]

Parents, as is appropriate, instruct and discipline their children. Therefore, when the second child is born, the first thinks, "Aha! Now is my chance!"

Recording artist Cynthia Clawson admitted to mercilessly dominating her younger sister, Patti. When a third child was born, Patti in turn exercised her power over him by sitting on him and biting him.

Younger siblings, in retaliation for being dominated, may seek revenge. They pester, they tease, they plot. Occasionally, when my older sisters were undressing, I'd run and hide in the hall closet which housed our laundry chute. I'd crouch on the shelf above, waiting breathlessly for the moment when one of them would unsuspectingly open the door. Then I'd leap out with a blood-curdling yell, stopping her heart and filling my own with temporary glee.

**Recovery is the norm**
And yet, studies show that most siblings find themselves getting closer as adults. On my fireplace mantle I have a faded black-and-white photograph of my sisters and me as wide-eyed little girls.

*Dee, Sally, Bonnie*

If our parents die before we do, and it is probable that they will, we will cling to one another for comfort. And if our husbands die before we do, and that could certainly happen, for widows outnumber widowers five to one, we again will desperately need one another. Our relationship as sisters may very well be the longest relationship of our lives; we yearn for it to be the best it can be. The older we get, the closer we move together emotionally.

Likewise, Cynthia Clawson and her sister Patti are soulmates, giving one another strength in their demanding life ministries. Cynthia said, "When something good happens to me, I want to pick up the phone and say, 'Hey Patti, listen to this!' or when something horrible happens, 'Patti, you are not going to believe what happened to me!' I know she's going to understand. It's kind of like talking to myself."

The saying, "Blood is thicker than water," implies that there is a richness in kin relationships which friends can never attain. Actually, I am convinced that, *in Christ,* friendships can be as deep as kin relationships. It is true, however, that shared genes, childhoods, bedrooms, and memories can tie you together in bonds that are not easily severed. And parents (and mentors) who help children to appreciate these bonds are laying the groundwork for long-lasting love.

## Shared genes

Sometimes when I laugh, or inflect my voice a certain way, I hear one of my sister's voices echoing back at me. My sisters and I are linked genetically. We have similar voices, a dramatic flair, and callouses on the bottoms of our left feet.

Sometimes we don't realize how much we are like a sibling until we are with people who know that sibling well. When I visited my sister Sally's Bible study in Austin, her friends kept smiling when I talked, not because I was humorous, but because my words and facial expressions reminded them so much of the friend they knew so well.

When my sisters and I fought as children, our dad would sit down and give us a complex mathematical theory that siblings shared more blood than any other relation — more, even, than parent and child. Then he would lean back in his chair, smile, and say, "So let's not have anymore quarreling among you — for you are sisters." This is exactly the peace-making plea Abraham used with Lot, when their herdsmen were quarreling over land. Abraham said, "Let's not have any quarreling between you and me, or between your herdsmen and mine, for we are brothers" (Genesis 13:8). I firmly believe that it is a wise parent who intercedes and encourages siblings to love each other and to become aware of the danger of careless words, words which can leave lifelong scars.

Often the most teachable moments are not during a quarrel, but during peacetime. If your children memorize passages dealing with relationship skills, those passages will guide them all of their lives. Our most successful runs at family devotions have been when we've acted out Proverbs.

Each parent takes a child or two, plans a proverb skit, and comes back to perform it. Here's a sample skit, based on Proverbs 15:1: "A gentle answer turns away wrath, but a harsh word stirs up anger."

SCENE 1:
>SALLY: Who ate all the cookies?
>ANNE: You should thank me, you're watching your weight!
>SALLY: [Pushes her] You little brat!

SCENE 2:
>SALLY: Who ate all the cookies?
>ANNE: I'm sorry! I should have left you one!
>SALLY: Oh, it's no big deal. [Hugs her]

We have a responsibility to train our children, not only to promote family harmony, but to prepare them for relationships for the rest of their lives. A sister is often your first roommate in life — but she won't be your last. Habits learned with her will affect all your future roommates!

**Shared bedrooms**
Shared bedrooms are a source of joy and pain, but always, of memories. Patti Clawson Berry says that she and her sister Cynthia had a blast: "Cynthia was a very imaginative storyteller, and we'd be under the covers with a flashlight. We had a tiny tape recorder and we'd make tapes until 2 in the morning."

As adults, Patti and Cynthia still share a hotel bedroom when they are on tour. Cynthia said, "And sometimes, when we were a little younger, we'd come back to the room with pent-up energy and jump on the bed!"

Shared bedrooms are also a source of strife. Cynthia and Patti fought over the invisible line in the bed, and complained, "Your pajamas are touching my pajamas!" Many a neatnik has been paired with a messy. Sometimes sisters long for their own space, their own identity. Jan Kiemel Ream, twin sister of Ann Kiemel Anderson, writes, in *Struggling for Wholeness:*

> Ann and I had not only spent nine months in the womb together but eighteen years in the same bedroom. . . . I honestly didn't know who "I" was. I probably knew better who Ann was. I had never walked out the door without her approval on what I was wearing and didn't know even how to roll my own hair.[2]

When we adopted five-year-old Anne from an orphanage in Korea, I envisioned her sharing a bedroom with our then eleven-year-old daughter, Sally (who is named after my sister, Sally). However, my plans went awry when Sally was overcome, not with tender sister feelings, but with rivalry. Articulately, she explained to me that she was not enjoying sharing a room with Anne, "Everybody thinks Anne is so darling! You can't possibly understand my pain, because you were always the baby. You can't imagine what it's like to be the baby for eleven years and then to be rudely displaced. I don't want to sleep next to her. Her breathing bugs me."

My husband and I prayed fervently for Sally and Anne's relationship. Just as girls who are friends may need a time of space from each other, I realized that can be true with sisters. So we fixed up a room in the basement for Sally, wallpapering and painting to her specifications. We also showered Sally with love and patience. In a year's time, great healing had taken place, and Sally was often inviting an excited Anne to come down and spend the night with her. The summer following I was swimming to the raft with Sally when she said, "Mom, I'm so glad we adopted Anne. There would be such a gaping hole in my life if I didn't have a sister."

*Annie & Sally*

Now Sally is seventeen, and openly shares that the terrible year in which she felt "displaced by Anne," and which kept her parents on their knees, was a spiritual turning point in her life.

"God revealed to me that my attitude was selfishness. He took my selfishness and turned it into a deep love for my sister and those like her who were hurting," she relates.

If your children are plagued with rivalry, *get on your knees and pray,* for we belong to a God who bends down and listens. The irritating sand of rivalry may bring forth a pearl — if you pray.

One of the comforts of adult sisterhood is getting past those mercurial years when your relationship fluctuates between warm intimacy and a glacial gap. For me, the gap between me and my sisters seemed enormous all through childhood. They were six and four when I was born, and I was the invader, the pesty (and I truly was) little sister who was always tattling, meddling, intruding. I remember, however, the day the gap closed. I became very ill one night when my parents were gone and Bonnie, who was about fourteen, was in charge. She was so concerned — calling the doctor and a neighbor, and getting me to the hospital emergency room. The warm feeling welling up inside of me wasn't just fever; it was the realization that my sister loved me.

My memories of magical moments were during that period when my sisters opened their circle and drew me in. Some of my best memories are from the summer, where we shared beds in a loft in our log cabin. With our parents talking below, the sound of the waves on the beach, and the light of the fire flickering against the wall, Sally, the eldest, mentored us. She whispered lessons on popularity: "When you get to high school, you will change classrooms between each period. When you pass people in the hall, smile, and say their names. Look right in their eyes and say, enthusiastically, 'Hi Susie!' and 'Hi John!' This will help you be popular!"

We soaked it in, and vowed to do as our sister, the Homecoming Queen, instructed.

Our log cabin was plagued with bats, which Sally told us could get tangled in our hair. I can remember sleeping under the sheet like spoons with Bonnie, my smaller body tucked into her protective one. I felt loved, cared for, shielded.

### Shared memories

One night when my parents were out, Sally narrated Edgar Allan Poe's "The Telltale Heart," with great dramatic flair. Soon we were hearing noises everywhere. To protect ourselves, we got out the metal marshmallow sticks which hung in a rack next to the fireplace. When our parents returned late that night, they opened the door to find their three daughters poised, ready to plunge those metal sticks into an intruder's telltale heart.

Patti and Cynthia Clawson used to pretend they were Roy Rogers and Trigger. Cynthia was Trigger (because that was the more powerful part) and Patti would put a rope in her mouth and lead her around the backyard. (Cynthia says,

"That's probably why I have capped teeth today.")

One of the conversations we often have at dinnertime is a sharing of memories — for in the telling and retelling, bonds are cemented. Likewise, bringing out the family movies and photo albums strengthens sibling bonds.

## Shared mother stories

My sisters and I often swap "mother stories" when we are together. Last summer we were remembering how Mother, a gifted soprano, would break into "Oh, What a Beautiful Morning" when we were out walking. We would all shrink several steps behind her. Mother stories bond us together. No one knows our mother like we do — and we are proud that we are related to such a creative and dazzling woman! And when one of us says to the other, "You are sounding just like Mother," we burst into laughter, knowing precisely what that means, and secretly proud that we, like Mother, will never be boring.

Author Anne Ortlund says that her mother was intensely a lady, and instructed her daughters in proper protocol, grooming, and manners. Anne writes of an experience she had with her sisters as adults: "We three sisters were in Washington, sitting on the grass watching a parade. It's been almost a half a century since Mother dressed us, but we discovered that for all our casual cottons, we had on skirts — and *hose*. We looked at one another, laughed, and acknowledged, 'Mother!' "[3]

## Shared spiritual strength

My sister Sally led me to Christ when I was a young mother. Sally had come to Christ a year before through the influence of Campus Crusade for Christ. God impressed on Sally's heart, in October of 1966, that I was more open to spiritual things than I had been in the past, and that she should travel to Indiana and lift up the claims of Christ. Though it was not a convenient time for her, she obeyed — and I am eternally grateful that she did.

Jennie Dimkoff, Carol Kent's younger sister, tells of walking out to the hayloft when she was seven, overwhelmed with doubts about her salvation: "I heard a noise and saw Carol, who was eleven, up in the hay mound having her devotions. To see her privately and quietly spending time with God was a real testimony to me. I climbed up next to her and poured out all my doubts and fears about my soul and she said, 'Jennie, just to be sure, let's pray together.' And she prayed with me, and from that day on I had assurance."

Jennie also tells of sharing a bedroom with Carol and of kneeling in prayer with her at night. "One prayer we prayed repeatedly was that others would be able to see Jesus on our faces. As adults, Carol and I began ministering together by singing at a retreat. Afterwards a woman came up and said, 'I can see Jesus on your faces.' The memory of our prayer as little girls came back instantly. And since that time there have been countless times people have told us that. God honored our prayer as children, and He continues to bond us together as adults."

### Shared sorrow
Because siblings have more years together than any other relatives, they are bound to share sorrow — for life is full of sorrow.

The Barrett Sisters, a black Gospel team, have sung together for over thirty years. When Delois's fourteen-year-old daughter became ill with hepatitis, and was suffering tremendously, Delois said, "The three of us joined hands around the bed and asked the Lord to quiet her down. We told God it was all right to take her and asked Him to let her slip away, and that's exactly what the Lord did."[4]

Bennie Wiley is the younger and only sister of Washington, D.C. Mayor Sharon Pratt Dixon. When Sharon was four and Bennie two, their father told them the news that their mother had died. He asked his daughters to promise him that they would "look out for each other, stick together, and never let anything or anyone come between them." Bennie says, "I remember the strength in Sharon's eyes . . . and from that day on, Sharon assumed responsibility for me. We have always been the constant in each other's lives."[5]

Most sisters are good friends, and a few become best friends. Yet rivalry is an underlying current in most sister relationships. For most, it's mild. For some, it's severe — and, as it was for Rachel and Leah of Genesis, their rivalry can be the obsession of their lives. Some sisters never grow up. They squabble until death parts them.

**In the next chapter . . .**
In beginning the section on putting away childish ways, let's begin with adult sisters. When Elizabeth Fishel, author of *Sisters,* researched women, she discovered that sisters longed to "unmask and disempower jealousy,"[6] for it still troubled most of them.

Is it really possible to completely outgrow sibling rivalry?

# Bible Study for Individuals or Small Groups

In the first two didactic passages, look at adjectives, comparisons, admonitions. In the Genesis narrative sections, remember the *Who? When? What? Where? How?* and *Why?* questions. Record observations and an application for each passage.

Psalm 133

Observations:

Principles to apply:

Application:

Proverbs 22:6

Observations:

Principles to apply:

Application:

Genesis 13:5-9

Observations:

Principles to apply:

Application:

Read the story of Joseph in Genesis 37–45. Then particularly observe the emotions in the following excerpts and ask: "Why so much intensity?" What application can you make?

Genesis 43:29-31

Observations:


Principles to apply:


Application:


Genesis 44:27-33

Observations:


Principles to apply:


Application:


Genesis 45:14-15

Observations:


Principles to apply:


Application:

# Part II

**When I became an adult,
I put an end to childish ways.**

1 Corinthians 13:11 (NRSVB)

*After all this time—you girls still don't*
*realize. Daddy's gone. One day I'll*
*be gone. Children will leave you. So*
*will husbands and lovers. You're the only*
*ones who know each other from cradle to grave.*

"Mama" in the television show "Sisters"

## six
# Can You Ever Outgrow Sibling Rivalry?

Most parents, when conceiving their children, don't project what their childrens' lives will be like in sixty years. Yet according to Dr. Stephen Bank and Dr. Michael Kahn, authors of *The Sibling Bond,* siblings provide a highly supportive network in old age, when parents and spouses have died, and children have gone their separate ways. The authors write:

> The decision made by a twentieth-century parent to have
> only one child can have consequences for life in the twen-
> ty-first century: the loneliest person in the world may well
> be the aged, unmarried only child who has no children and
> no siblings to love or be loved by.[1]

The sibling bond tends to be much more enduring than most friendships: only 3 percent of siblings permanently disconnect. Jan, a young professional woman, describes what her siblings meant to her during the death of her mother: "It was a great comfort to be with my older brother and sister, to be with the people grieving the same loss I was. I had a real sense of going through that family crisis *together*. And a week later, when Christmas came, I realized that even with my mother gone (the woman who 'made' Christmas for us all) I still had family to come home to. And I know we'll continue to get together even after my father dies. At times like this, I'm glad I'm not an only child."

Yet many who are blessed with siblings do *not* relate well to them. Experts say that failure to overcome rivalry separates siblings more than any factor.

Rivalry, in the Latin, means "having rights to the same stream." For siblings, that stream is the parents' love and approval. When I was pregnant with our second child I feared, as is common with mothers, that I might not love my second child as much as my first. My love for my firstborn was *so* overwhelming that I feared there might not be enough love left in my heart for another. Yet when Johnny was born, my love welled up and overflowed. And today, as the mother of five, I believe that if God gives you a child, He also supplies plenty of love for each child.

However, some parents play favorites because of emotional problems of their own. Carolyn Koons, who was raised in an abusive home, felt the force of her father's hatred because he knew he was not her biological father. Every time he looked at her, he was reminded of his wife's infidelity.

One year he bought her brothers new bikes for their birthdays and then went to the dump to find the worst bike he could to give to Carolyn.

If a parent plays favorites, the deprived children are impacted severely. Parents who continually overvalue one child provide the fuel for long-lasting sibling rivalry, even, Bank says, "reaching back from the grave."[2]

Ginny, who checks my groceries, slid my food over the scanner a week before Christmas and vented her emotion: "I hate the holidays. My parents not only loved my brother best growing up, they still do. When we go home, he'll have the spotlight. His kids will get elaborate gifts. Mine will get socks. And yet I keep going home, hoping it will be different."

If you grew up in a family where parents played favorites, your challenge is greater — but not insurmountable.

**Overcoming the pain of favoritism**

Jacob and Esau were victims of parental favoritism and suffered enormously. Esau articulates that pain when he discovers that his father has given his blessing to his brother, and cries, weeping: "Bless me — me too, my father!" (Genesis 27:34)

In *The Blessing,* John Trent and Gary Smalley say that Esau's anguished cry is being echoed today by many: "Some will try to break down the door to their parents' hearts to receive this missed blessing, but all too often their attempt fails. For whatever reason, they have to face the fact that their blessing will have to come from another source.[3]

Sometimes parental favoritism is perceived rather than real. As a mother of five, I know how difficult it is to treat each child equally. After we adopted Anne, I searched the catalogs for a Christmas stocking. I was delighted to find one which matched the style of our other children's stockings! However, when it arrived, Sally held it up to her own and found Anne's to be two inches longer. Accusingly she turned to me and asked, "Why is Anne's stocking bigger?" My patience ran thin, and Sally still remembers that I reacted by saying, "Give me a break!"

My husband has helped me to see that, even if a child's feeling of being slighted are imagined, it is best to treat her fears with respect, or you may aggravate the rivalry. During that difficult year of Sally's adjustment, Steve told me, repeatedly, "Even though Sally's fears of losing our love are unreasonable, they don't feel that way to her. If we are patient, I think she'll get past it, and I think the dividend will be that she and Anne will be close."

He was right. I have become more compassionate toward the child who feels the loss of losing the limelight, even though it is temporary. Author Adrianne Rich said, "When my sister was born, it was like losing the Garden of Eden."[4] A child's whole world is his or her parents' love, and it *is* a shock suddenly to have to share it.

Most children *are* favored for a temporary period, and that is not necessarily wrong. A wise parent keeps communicating that this perceived favoritism is temporary, and keeps showering love on the child who is hurting.

Carol Kent told me, "My brother Ben was born in the middle of the night. After four girls, Dad was euphoric. He ran up the stairs to our big second story bedroom, waking us with his shout: 'It's a boy! It's a boy! And Benjamin means SON OF MY RIGHT HAND!' "

Yet despite the fact that Ben seemed, at least for the time, to be the favored child, the sisters felt joy, not rivalry. Each felt loved and cherished and was therefore able to rejoice in their brother's birth.

Rivalry is natural, but not desirable. I still have greater feelings of rivalry toward my sisters than I do toward my friends. When Bonnie's son went to Yale, I felt a tremor of jealousy and dallied with the temptation to encourage my

*The Clyde Afman Family*

children to go to Ivy League schools. I am so thankful that knowing Christ and His Word helps me to veer away from choices based on rivalry.

Outgrowing sibling rivalry helps us make better choices for our lives, but, more than that, fills our lives with a richness of relationship that is likely to last into old age.

Here are some ways that have been helpful to me and to others in putting away childish ways.

### Admitting feelings of envy

Counselor Tara Markey believes that talking about childhood feelings is essential for healing: "You have to let down your guard. It becomes a trust issue — trust that you aren't going to hurt me like you did when I was a kid."[5] A few years ago I admitted my feelings of envy about not being a Homecoming Queen to my sisters, and our conversation brought great healing to me. Bonnie said, "I certainly hope that becoming Homecoming Queen is not going to be my ultimate achievement in life." We laughed and I began to look at that time, not with pain, but with perspective and with humor.

Ann Kiemel's twin sister, Jan Ream, honestly shared that, while Ann had all the fame of an author and speaker, Jan at least felt she excelled in the area of marriage and motherhood. In *Struggling for Wholeness,* Jan writes:

> When Ann married Will Anderson, it brought with it the most traumatic pain I had ever felt. It was during their honeymoon when I finally realized the bottom of my pain lay in the fact that . . . she had seemingly always beaten me in any task we set out to conquer. . . . Now she was entering those two turfs [marriage and motherhood] and she would certainly supersede me again.[6]

For Ann and Jan, much healing has come about simply because they have been willing to admit their rivalry. Jan says,

> For years I denied that I ever competed with Ann. But today I ashamedly admit that the feelings are there. In reality, if women were honest, all would confess to it. . . . I don't think we ever get rid of the struggle and pain of unhealthy competing. . . . Rather I think our freedom comes when we can confess it.[7]

## Looking for God's approval

Jennie Dimkoff says that people often marvel that she doesn't feel jealous of her sister, Carol Kent. Jennie and Carol have parallel lives in many ways, including the fact that they each speak to women's groups nearly every weekend — but Carol's star is higher, right now, than is Jennie's. I was deeply moved by what Jennie told me: "I've pondered the story of Miriam — and of how, though she was gifted, she was still critical and jealous of her specially anointed brother, Moses. And God punished her (Numbers 12). After that, the only thing we are told about Miriam is to 'remember what God did to Miriam' (Deuteronomy 24:9). Actually, what we do remember is her standing by the reeds watching Moses in his basket, or dancing with a tambourine after the parting of the Red Sea. But *God* tells us to remember how she was jealous and how He punished her. When I look at Carol, not only is she my best friend and my kindred spirit, but God has especially anointed her. There have been times when I sit back in awe at what God is doing through her. And it makes me cry. It would be so sinful and wrong to be jealous of her.''

It grieves God when we cannot be content with how He has gifted us, but instead covet the gifts of a sibling. Karen Mains and Valerie Bell are gifted sisters who work closely together on ''The Chapel of the Air,'' and do it well. Once, on the broadcast, Karen said:

> Eric Liddell, the hero of *Chariots of Fire,* said that he ran because God made him fast, and he felt God's pleasure when he ran. When we feel the intimate pleasure of God, it doesn't matter how he chooses to work with our brothers and sisters.[8]

## Show your siblings how much you care

In Proverbs 21:14, we're told that a gift can soothe anger. When Jacob returned home, a mature and broken man, he was eager to reconcile with Esau. The gifts that he sent ahead were his way of apologizing and expressing love to the brother he had wronged.

It's amazing how much healing the expression of love provides. Bonnie, the sister closest to my age, was my greatest rival. Bonnie showed me how much she cared for me by flying to Nebraska and organizing a surprise twenty-fifth wedding anniversary celebration for Steve and me. There were many toasts that weekend, but the one I'll never forget was from Bonnie. With her eyes flooding with tears, she raised her glass of juice and said, ''Dee, I want you to know how very very precious you are to me and how much I love you.''

It's amazing how that toast melted away nearly all of my rivalry!

In addition to longing for a "blessing" from our parents, most of us long for a "blessing" from our siblings as well. We want to know that we are loved and special in their eyes. Last year we adopted a third daughter, who is between the ages of Sally and Anne. Shortly after we brought Beth home, we found Anne upstairs weeping on her bed. The pain she was feeling that day was not only from the fact that we, her parents, had been giving Beth extra attention, but that Sally, Anne's big sister, had had Beth in her room trying on clothes all evening. The next morning Sally took Anne (and only Anne) out for donuts before school as a way of saying, "I love you Anne—always."

## Affirming your siblings

Carol Kent told me, "I think it's really important to look at your siblings and find something that they do well and brag on it. Most human beings, especially women, suffer from low self-esteem. You could have been raised in the best Christian family possible and still be struggling with feelings of inadequacy. When my first book came out, my four sisters celebrated with me, through letters and calls! Jennie carried my books to her speaking engagements and told people 'This is the best book I've ever read in my whole life and you need to get it today.' "

Outgrowing sibling rivalry is a worthwhile pursuit. Jan Senn, who described herself as "the brat little sister who always interrupted the boyfriends in the basement to iron my ribbons" has made peace with her older brother and sister. Today, they're helping each other fill the gap that the loss of their mother has created. Reflectively, Jan said, "Mom was Karen's best friend, and they'd spend hours just talking on the phone, but Karen and I always had a purpose when we talked to each other. After Mom's death, however,

Karen called me and was chatting on and on, and I kept thinking, 'What's the point of this call?' and then a warm feeling welled up inside me as I realized there wasn't a point. She just wanted to talk."

There is *so very much* to be gained by outgrowing sibling rivalry.

Likewise, there is much to be gained by putting away childish ways in our friendships.

After I spoke at "The Changed Life Seminar" near Toledo about "Putting away Childish Ways," a threesome came up to me. A pretty brunette in the middle was the first to speak, thanking me profusely for thoughts I had shared. The young woman on her left said, "This has been a very challenging retreat! A painfully maturing one!"

I raised my eyebrows — I wanted further explanation!

The woman in the middle hugged the friend who'd made herself vulnerable and explained, "Lilly didn't think you could have more than one best friend."

I smiled, as I suddenly realized the significance of the threesome.

**In the next chapter . . .**
Three doesn't work very well with little girls — but it *should* work with women. It's time to learn to put away childish ways in friendship. Next let's consider how to make a threesome work.

# Bible Study for Individuals or Small Groups

Read the historical account, remembering the narrative questions of *Who? What? Why? How?* etc.

Genesis 27:30-46

Observations:


Principles to apply:


Application:


Genesis 33:8-11

Observations:


Principles to apply:


Application:


Numbers 12

Observations:


Principles to apply:


Application:

*Maybe it's crazy, but when my best
friend began to pull away a little,
I felt more like a jilted lover than a
friend who'd been knocked down a notch
or two in importance. It wasn't good
enough to be just one of her close friends,
not after what we shared for so many years.*

A fifty-year-old woman from *Just Friends*[1]

seven

# The Triangle

Though it's been thirty-eight years, the tearful scene between Judy, the new girl in my fifth grade, and Donna and me, who were best friends, is indelibly impressed on my guilty heart.

I was drawn to Judy the moment Miss Kolander introduced her to our class. She looked just like one of my dolls:

wispy black curls framing a petite porcelain face with huge blue eyes — and she dimpled when she smiled, which was often. When Judy called me that week and asked if *I* could come and spend an overnight with her on Friday, I was elated to be the chosen one! And I was not disappointed. We roasted hot dogs and marshmallows in her family room fireplace and sat on a blanket while I told her all about who was nice and who wasn't in the fifth grade. That night we whispered and giggled under the covers until it was very late, savoring the joy of friendship discovered.

*But Donna was my best friend — and Donna was angry that I had spent the night at Judy's.* Donna threw down the gauntlet: I had to choose. I couldn't have them both. I chose Donna — because Donna had been my best friend for two years. We were a constant in each other's lives: we played at every recess, walked home together every night, and talked on the phone when we were apart. I didn't think I could survive without Donna. I was forced to let Judy know my decision on Monday when she caught up with Donna and me after school. Her deep dimples and sparkling blue eyes told me she was unsuspecting of the treachery that was coming. I can still remember where we stood on the sidewalk outside of McClain Grade School when Donna announced, "Dee and I are going to walk home together."

"But can't I walk with you too?" asked Judy.

Hesitantly, I replied, "I'm sorry."

"But I thought we were getting to be good friends!" exclaimed Judy.

I paused. I felt so torn! Donna took my hand possessively. "Judy, I really am sorry — but Donna is my best friend."

"My mother says that three girls can be good friends. Can't we all be friends?" asked Judy.

My concern was rising. Judy's mother had been wonderful to me on Friday night, telling me she was so glad Judy had such a nice little friend. Donna, sensing my vacillating heart, stepped dramatically forward, placing herself between Judy and me.

"Judy, you can't have more than one best friend! Dee and I were best friends before you ever came here. So you have to find a different best friend."

"Dee?" Judy's lip was trembling now. She looked at me beseechingly as Donna turned and cast me a warning look.

Cowardly, I responded, "Donna is my best friend."

Defeated, Judy cried, "I hate you both! You are both so mean! I never want to play with you again!" She fled, in tears.

I would like to tell you that when I became a woman I put away childish ways — but it took a while for me to see the sin in territorial friendships. But today I see it clearly! (And wherever you are, Judy — please forgive me!)

I'd like to share with you some of the ways God has changed my thinking.

### The new kid on the block

When I was growing up, my parents never moved. I spent my first eighteen years in the same house on Highland View Drive in West Bend, Wisconsin. I was never the new kid on the block — and, as you can see from the story above, I was not particularly compassionate toward her plight!

After I married, however, Steve and I moved *eight* times because each new venture of his medical training or time in the Public Health Service took him to a different region of the United States. I quickly learned what it meant to be the new kid looking in on those who were content in their existing network of friendships!

God, in His grace, didn't treat me as I had treated others in my childhood. When we moved to Fargo, North Dakota, I prayed for a soulmate — as I had learned to do! I was doing interviews for a writing project and one of the most interesting women I interviewed was Ann Dahl. I was immediately attracted to her depth and warmth, and we had an interchange that day that made me feel that she might be the friend for whom I longed. Something I said caused Ann to smile and say: "You sound a bit like an evangelical feminist! Are you?"

Like a diver who's reluctant to dive into untested waters, I paused. Quickly I reassured my new acquaintance that I was pro-life, pro-family, and pro-male! Smiling empathetically, she said: "I'm somewhere between Marabel Morgan's *Total Woman* and Letha Scanzoni's *All We're Meant to Be*."

I suddenly sensed, as Anne of Green Gables is fond of saying, "a kindred spirit." She was a reader, a ponderer! I laughed and said, "I'm somewhere in there too!" Then I freely shared some of the concepts I had learned from various authors who held the high view of Scripture, yet felt that some Christian views of marriage and of ministry failed to appreciate that God intended women to be active participants. Ann was familiar with those authors and we began finishing each other's sentences. I shared the pain I had felt in one denomination when I realized that women were not welcome to share their thoughts in Sunday School class. Ann was completely compassionate. We experienced the joy of seeing our friendship sprout before our very eyes.

A few months later, Ann told me that her very best friend from the past was moving from Florida to Fargo! Though I smiled on the outside, I was sure this new friendship, which had sprung up so quickly, was in danger of being crowded out in its infancy, before it had a chance to grow strong and tall. Ann raved about Sylvia and her husband Kendall, who was coming to work with Ann's husband. Kendall and Howie had been close since their days together at Trinity Seminary. Not only were Sylvia and Ann soulmates, their husbands were as well! I felt the cold wind approaching: Sylvia and Ann would be as snug as bugs in a rug — and I would be outside, shivering in the bitter Fargo winter!

But that isn't what happened. Ann also raved to Sylvia about me and arranged for the three of us to have lunch together. Sylvia didn't seem threatened by me in the least — just terribly eager to meet me! Our time together that day was one of the most special fellowships in my memory. Sparks went from one to another as we sharpened one another with our understanding of Scripture, and of thoughts from various Christian authors. Laughter abounded. Afterwards we walked and prayed together — experiencing the joy of a threefold cord.

### Helping each other find strength in God

Author Gail McDonald helped me to see a key verse in the friendship of David and Jonathan. When David was hiding at Horesh, in fear of being murdered by King Saul, Jonathan went to him and "helped him find strength in God" (1 Samuel 23:16). Gail asked, "Do you help your friend find strength in you? Or in God?" How wise Jonathan was! Shortly after this he was killed in battle, but David was not abandoned, for his strength was in God.

I believe that Jonathan helped David find strength in God by praying with him, by encouraging him with Scripture, and by sharing the way he saw God working. This kind of friendship was the kind of friendship I experienced with Ann and Sylvia. Rather than behaving like little girls, guarded and territorial concerning their best friend, they opened their circle. They were convinced that God was leading the three of us to be friends. And when we got together, we helped each other find strength, not in each other, but in God. Our friendship was healthy, edifying, and satisfying. I knew that Ann and Sylvia would always be closer to each other than either was to me, because their friendship had such deep roots. But I was deeply grateful that they had opened their circle and drew me in. If I spent time with one and not the other, there was no jealousy — just delight in our threefold cord!

When we parted a year later (because Steve and I were moving to Nebraska), though it *was* painful, it wasn't devastating. God was going with me — and I felt He would provide me with soulmates in Nebraska as He had in Fargo. My security was not in Ann and Sylvia, but in God.

After I moved, I urged Ann to call the Fargo telephone company and inquire about conference calls so that the three of us could talk simultaneously. Ann called a man at Bell Telephone. After discovering that two of the parties lived in Fargo, he gently asked, "Ma'am — do you have more than one telephone in your home?"

The light went on in Ann's head and, humiliated, she said, "Oh — my friend could pick up the extension!"

The man said, "Yes, Ma'am."

When Ann and Sylvia (who was on the extension) relayed this story to me, we howled.

One spring I was giving a retreat in Florida for Campus Crusade Staff women, and Sylvia (who now lives back in Florida) and Ann (who, in God's great timing, was visiting Sylvia that week!) came. After my last session, we headed to Daytona Beach for a walk along the ocean. As it happened, it was also "Bikers' Week" — so it wasn't quite the peaceful setting we had envisioned. Along with swooping seagulls and lapping waves were roaring motorcyclists. Yet the rumble of the motors didn't keep us from connecting. We shouted to be heard, and grinned — grins born not only of the humor of our situation, but of the deep joy of being reunited and of helping one another, once again, find strength in God.

### A cord of three strands

Because as women we have a tendency toward dependency, having two soulmates may be a safeguard. It's a bit too easy, when you have just one soulmate, to become all things to each other, and to put unreasonable demands on each other.

I feel that God has given me a "composite" soulmate where I live now in a few very good friends. Because I have more than one soulmate, I am less demanding. When a friend needs space for family or ministry, I am more willing to give it. And when I need space, I feel less like I am abandoning my friends, for I know that they have other sources of emotional nurturing. Solomon says, in Ecclesiastes 4:9, that two are better than one. He goes on, in verse 12, to say, "Though one may be overpowered, two can defend themselves. A cord of three strands is not quickly broken."

While a cord of three strands is often likened to two friends and God (which is an apt analogy), there's also support here for having more than one soulmate. And it may very well be healthier! One woman who has been delivered from a lesbian relationship called me to thank me for *The Friendships of Women* and its part in helping her. She told me, "I always realized the sexual involvement was sin, but I didn't know how to be delivered. Your book helped me to see the root problem was dependency — we had transferred our dependency from God to each other."

This woman is back on track. To stay there, not only does she need to keep her love relationship with the Lord alive, she needs to be on guard about becoming dependent on any one woman ever again. One of the best ways to do that is by having more than one close friend.

**In the next chapter . . .**
I have counseled many a young wife that she needs to have other close friends in addition to her husband. Expecting a husband to be "all things" to you can be damaging to your marriage.

But what do you do if your husband is threatened by your friendships?

# Bible Study for Individuals or Small Groups

Look for commands, comparisons, key phrases, and words.

Ecclesiastes 4:9-12

Observations:

Meaning:

Application:

Romans 1:18-32

Observations:

Meaning:

Application:

1 Samuel 23:15-18

Observations:

Meaning:

Application:

### eight
# Husbands versus Best Friends

Psychotherapist Lillian Rubin explains that best friendships
may become a source of conflict with a mate because, especially in the beginning of a friendship, the intensity of the attach-
ment and the aura of romance surrounding a best friendship
can seem threatening to the exclusivity of the marriage
commitment. One man, whom she interviewed, said:

> She thinks I don't like her friend Peg, but that's not it.
> *(Uncomfortably)* I guess maybe I'm jealous. When they
> first met, you'd think they were having some kind of a
> love affair the way they were always trying to figure out
> ways to get together and talking on the phone all the time.
> Why would I feel good about that?[1]

Many men have never experienced a deep same-sex
friendship, and the intensity of a woman's relationship with
a best friend may perplex them.

After a man has been married for a while, he is aware that
his wife is not unusual in her need for deep same-sex friendships. Just being privy to a conversation between three
women is enough to educate him. Television talk show host-
ess Kathie Lee described the conversation she had with two
women friends and her husband, Frank Gifford.

> The four of us began sharing our private thoughts on love
> and relationships. . . . Then the woman-talk got so emo-
> tionally intimate, so intense and deeply spiritual, that
> Frank got up. Guess he couldn't stand the heat so he went
> back into the kitchen — after sweetly clearing the dishes.
> "I'll just leave you ladies alone," he said.[2]

In some cultures men *do* have close friendships with
other men. I received a fascinating letter from a woman
named Addy Mull, an American living in Africa. She wrote:
"Where I live, the men walk hand in hand, they kiss when
they greet, and after a soccer game they will often agree that
both teams won — because they feel that competition
hinders intimacy."

I also think that men, even in America, who are extremely
mature in Christ have experienced some of the intimate fellowship that the first disciples experienced. When a man's
security is firmly in Christ, he becomes less concerned about
status and is therefore more willing to make himself vulnerable, even to other men.

But for most men, same-sex intimacy is not a part of their lives. Their only confidante is their wives, and they are dependent upon her to meet their needs for deep friendship.

### Putting your husband first

The movie *Beaches* portrays a lifelong friendship between Rosalie, a flamboyant showgirl, and Susan, a quiet conservative. As adults, Rosalie and Susan have a particularly bitter fight in a department store. Later, Rosalie is convinced she has lost Susan. Grieving, she says to her husband: "What will I do without a best friend?"

In an attempt to comfort her, he says, "But you've got me."

Rosalie shakes her head and stares out into the distance. "It's not the same," she says, adamantly.

I think there are better ways of communicating your need for women friends to your husband. He must know that he is first, that no one can fill his place in your life, but that you also need women friends. A woman who has a same-sex confidante is not less likely to be close to her husband, as he might think, and it doesn't hurt to reassure him. A study by P. O'Connor found no association between the existence of friends who were confidantes and the respondents' level of confiding in their husbands.[3]

You can *show* your husband that your women friends are not going to detract from your marriage by giving priority to your time together as a couple. Most women are not going to be wounded if you are protective of your time with your husband. My friends are very gracious when they call and I ask them if I can call them back because Steve is home. If your friends don't understand, you may need to gently help them see that to be committed to you, you need them to be committed to your marriage as well.

If a friend seems jealous of your time with your husband, or if she makes derogatory remarks about him, beware. Several years ago a woman I'll call Jenna began writing me about feeling caught between loyalty to her husband and loyalty to her best friend, Nicole.

> I have never connected with anyone that way I've connected with Nicole. And she's always been there for me, even to the extent of flying to Mexico when I was in a car accident and nursing me back to health.
>
> When I started dating Frank, she told me it was THE MISTAKE OF MY LIFE. I was hurt, but I loved him and thought Nicole would grow to appreciate him. She hasn't! Though I married him, Nicole still tells me, constantly, that God has someone better for me.

It was clear to me from Jenna's letters that she needed to risk losing Nicole if Nicole couldn't be supportive of her marriage. Yet, though Jenna seemed to realize that Nicole was hurting her perception of Frank, she lacked the courage to take a stand. She wrote, wistfully, "I just can't lose Nicole. She's too important to me."

I believe that God, in His grace, intervened. For after a particularly sharp disagreement, *Nicole* called off the friendship. Jenna wrote me during that time, her letters filled with pain. "I miss her so much," she wrote, "when will I stop hurting?"

Years later Jenna came to one of my retreats and sought me out. She told me that, after Nicole retreated, she and Frank went to a Christian marriage counselor for sixteen months. In time, their marriage flourished. Now, with her priorities straight, she and Nicole were tentatively exploring renewing their friendship.

Reflectively, Jenna said: "Though the pain of having my best friend turn from me was intense, I now see that God meant it for our good. We had become inordinately important to each other and the Lord had to shake up our priorities. Today we each have other close friends.

"I now clearly see that any person outside of a marriage that encourages the breakup of a family unit without any scriptural basis is out of God's will. I am strong enough now to ask Nicole to respect my personhood and my relationship with the Lord enough to change her belief about Frank. If she can't, I will treasure my memories with her, but our friendship has no future."

There have been times when *I* have thought that my friends made a poor choice of a husband, *but because I value the sanctity of marriage, I need to be supportive of that marriage!* The only exception to this is when, because of a husband's substance abuse, physical abuse, or infidelity, you need to give your friend the support she needs to separate from him and exercise tough love, the kind of love that says, "I love you — but I will not tolerate this behavior. Therefore we can't be together unless you get the help you need to make a genuine change."

### Supporting your friend's marriage

As I shared in the opening chapter of this book, studies show that women's friendships generally enhance rather than hurt marriages. As Christians, that should be doubly true, as we know how highly God values the sanctity of marriage. It isn't our responsibility to point out the faults of our friend's husband.

But what do you do when it's your friend who is pointing out her husband's faults? Dr. Dobson asked me about this tricky situation when I was on "Focus on the Family." He said, "On the one hand, she needs to respect her husband — on the other hand, in a true friendship, she needs to be able to ventilate. What's the solution?"

I think we should be able to ventilate, but only to friends who understand the sanctity of marriage. And when a friend is ventilating to me, I must keep *uppermost* in my mind that

I want the best for her, and the best is a response which will edify her marriage. Sometimes I can help diffuse emotion by letting her ventilate, sometimes I can help her to see his side, and sometimes I can help her see the humor in the situation.

One summer, Margaret and Larry and their three children stopped to visit me and our children at our summer place. (My husband had not yet joined us.) Larry, an administrator, is like many left-brained, goal-oriented men. He had scheduled their "vacation" tightly—they were going to "conquer" ten places in ten days! When the five of them arrived at our cabin (their fifth goal), I sensed the tension between Margaret and Larry.

I hurried them out to the dock to catch a glimpse of the scarlet sun slipping into the bay, because they planned to leave in the morning, and I thought it might be their only Door County sunset. When just a crimson hue remained, the chill drove us inside to the fire. Margaret collapsed in a big chair, but Larry was restless and decided to take the children miniature golfing.

Alone together, I empathized with my friend: "Marg, is your vacation wearing you out?"

"Oh, yes! We've been going so hard. I would love to take it easy, but Larry has all these goals he wants to accomplish!"

I laughed, hoping to defuse her tension with humor. I told her that Larry reminded me of my wonderful dad, who took months meticulously preparing for family trips and had every moment carefully scheduled. A few years ago, though he was in his late 70s, Dad whirled my mother, Steve, and me through every corner of England and Scotland in ten days. I often was aware, during that trip, of the differences between men and women. Dad wanted us to see all the famous spots; Mother wanted to meander through the shops, sit down, have tea, and talk. I was feeling somewhat frustrated about the trip until, one night, I saw my dad poring over his careful plans for the next day. My heart filled with love for him as I realized how hard he was working. The next day we let Mother and Steve rest at the hotel, while Dad and I explored Oxford together, seeing where C.S. Lewis taught, and lunched, and was buried. I told Margaret I cherished the memory of that joyous day with my dad — but I'd have missed it had God not helped me to see Dad's loving motives.

Margaret pensively poked at the fire. Smiling, she began reminiscing how she and Larry had reacted differently when their family was snowed in last winter.

"I absolutely love it when it snows so hard that Larry's office is closed and school is canceled. The family is cloistered together and the world is held at bay! When that happened last year, Larry made a big fire, like this one, and I envisioned playing games with the kids with a big bowl of popcorn. I was delighted to see the snow piling up because the five of us would be cozy in our circle of love before the flickering fire. It would be just like a scene from 'Little House on the Prairie.'

"Instead, Larry was excited about using his new snowblower. I suggested he wait until it stopped snowing and play a few games with us. But he just had to get out with his machine.

"I kept going to the window to see if he was nearly done, but when he finished our walk, I saw him across the street doing the neighbors' walks! Then, because it was still snowing, he started all over again."

When Larry and the children returned, they found us giggling. Taking his jacket off, Larry said, "I don't know if my ears are burning from the cold or because you two have been talking about me!"

We laughed at his discernment. I told him how much we appreciated the quiet time he'd given us together while he entertained the children. He responded, sensitively: "Well, I think Margaret needed that."

I gave him an appreciative smile and said, "Marg and I are so blessed to have discerning husbands like you and Steve. You are right — Marg does need to unwind! And you are right that we've been talking about you — and about the differences between men and women in general!"

Larry raised his eyebrows. "I think I'd better hear this."

We laughed, and I attempted an explanation: "Well, I think God designed most men to be goal-oriented, and most women to be relational — and sometimes that causes a bit of conflict! Like on days when the family is snowed in — or on vacations!"

Larry smiled good-naturedly, understanding my point. I seized the moment and said, "Larry, instead of getting back on the road tomorrow after breakfast, why not make it your goal to let Marg and the kids stop and catch their breath here! Call and cancel your reservations in Milwaukee. I'd absolutely love to have you for an extra day!"

The kids chorused, "Please, Dad!"

Larry laughed, putting his hands up in mock defense: "Well, tell you what — I'll think about it."

The next day we were graced from above with glorious weather. Encouraged by the warmer weather and the sight of our children skipping pebbles together on a sunlit bay, I gingerly made my plea again. Larry set his breakfast coffee mug down and grinned: "OK — we'll stay!" We rejoiced and ran to tell the kids, who rejoiced with us!

Sitting in a deck chair was too sedentary for Larry, but Margaret and I stretched out while he and their sons paddled the canoe to Horseshoe Island. (One of Larry's goals was to get a rock from each place they visited, and he decided a rock from an island would add character to their collection!) Margaret and I basked in the sun and watched her conquerers head for the island. We talked about how thankful we were to be married to conquerers, even though it could be frustrating. (Steve has conquered medical school, our taxes, our leaking roof, and the red tape involved in adopting children from other countries.) I could also give Margaret hope (for we are older than they) because I have seen Steve become much more relaxed and relational in his maturity.

When we saw Larry and the boys paddling home, we were concerned because the canoe was low in the water. We understood why when we saw the *boulder* they had retrieved for the rock collection. What a conquest! Marg and I couldn't stop laughing.

In her thank-you note, Margaret said the atmosphere of their vacation took a positive U-turn after their time at our summer place! How encouraged I felt to know I'd played a small part in strengthening their marriage!

**In the next chapter . . .**
Having a good, strong marriage isn't easy in this day of sexual infidelity, dual career marriages, and quick divorces. However, we do have one advantage that wives in Old Testament days lacked. Most of us don't have to worry about sharing our husbands with another wife or two.

Or do we?

# Bible Study for Individuals or Small Groups

Look for commands, comparisons, and key phrases and words. What application could there be in each of these passages for strengthening a friend's marriage?

1 Corinthians 13:1-8

Observations:

Meaning:

Application:

Proverbs 31:10-12, 26-31

Observations:

Meaning:

Application:

# Husbands versus Best Friends

Proverbs 20:5-6

Observations:

Meaning:

Application:

1 Timothy 5:13-14

Observations:

Meaning:

Application:

*I had lost my mate, and to some extent*
*my social position. I know my wife-in-law*
*[husband's new wife] is much better off*
*financially than I am. She's the one taking the*
*fancy trips and redecorating her home*
*while I'm pinching pennies.*
*But one thing I wasn't prepared for was my*
*five-year-old daughter coming to me*
*one day and saying, "Oh, Mommy,*
*Mara makes the best fried chicken, and*
*we had so much fun planting a garden*
*together. I can't wait to go back next Saturday."*

Anne Cryster, *The Wife-in-Law Trap*[1]

nine
# Can an Ex-wife and a New Wife Get Along?

Before Christ came to earth, many a woman had to share her husband with another wife. But Jesus elevated the position of women, and, for the next nineteen centuries, polygamy was rare.

In the middle of the twentieth century, however, divorce became first acceptable and then common. Today many

women are faced with stress similar to that of their polyga-
mous ancestors, because of the contemporary practice of
"serial" monogamy. Many women have become victims of
divorce just as women in the past were victims of polygamy.
Ann Cryster has coined the term "wife-in-law" to describe
the relationship between the ex-wife and the new wife. If
you are not a "wife-in-law," you probably have a friend who
is and who'd appreciate empathy and encouragement from
you.

PAIN is what is expressed over and over again by ex-
wives. The pain of the actual divorce is the beginning. But as
long as her other half remains single, she has hope of reconciliation, of the healing of her gaping wound. That's why the
news of a new wife is so devastating. One woman described
the shock like this: "The news of my ex's new wife? It's like
remembering where you were when Kennedy was shot."[2]

If you were the one who initiated the divorce, as was the
case with a friend of mine, you may assume you can get him
back if you choose. My friend kept telling me she was glad
she had divorced her husband. I half-believed her until I saw
how she reacted when he remarried. The reality that she
could never have him back sent her reeling.

First meetings with the new wife are typically traumatic,
says author Ann Cryster. She tells how one ex-wife felt the
first time she met her husband's new wife, Trish.

> I was working around the house that afternoon. Hank,
> Trish, and the kids had been away for Labor Day, and they
> suddenly pulled into the driveway. After eight hours in
> the car, Trish hops out in perfectly pressed linen shorts
> with every hair on her head in place. I felt like Godzilla
> facing Venus. It was the first time I had seen them as a
> couple, a family. I thought I had a grip on it all, but when I
> went back into the house I cried for the entire night. I
> can't describe the loneliness, the unhappiness. I was con-
> vinced that no one would ever love me again. I felt used
> up, discarded and ridiculous.[3]

I imagine that those were some of the feelings that Leah had when, after one week with her new husband, she saw her beautiful younger sister, Rachel, invade her tent. If there is one word to describe the lives of Leah and Rachel, it is PAIN.

## Leah: the rejected wife

Although mothers often get the rap for trying to manipulate marriages, in this story it's the father who's to blame. Laban veiled his older daughter Leah heavily so that Jacob would think he was marrying her beautiful younger sister, Rachel. All night long Jacob thought he was making love to Rachel. (Did he murmur softly, "Rachel, O, Rachel. . . "? ) But when dawn broke and he looked upon the face of his sleeping bride, Jacob realized he'd been duped. He tore from their tent to confront Laban, shouting: "Give me my wife. My time is completed, and I want to lie with her" (Genesis 29:21). Jacob had not only been deprived of sleeping with Rachel, he had been humiliated by thinking that he had! He probably felt like the laughingstock of Haran. And when Leah saw his reaction, she must have felt mortified, discarded.

Laban tried to placate Jacob, saying, "It is not our custom here to give the younger daughter in marriage before the older one. Finish this daughter's bridal week; then we will give you the younger one also, in return for another seven years of work" (Genesis 29:26-27).

So Leah had Jacob to herself for one week — a week in which he pined for Rachel.

When Rachel moved into their tent a week later, perhaps Leah fantasized that, after Jacob knew Rachel as she did, he wouldn't be so smitten. But he was. Throughout his life he adored Rachel. Even when Rachel was barren, Jacob loved her. And when she finally gave birth to Joseph, he was Jacob's favorite son, setting off ripples of sibling rivalry. Oh, the pain Leah endured all her life!

A friend of mine whom I will call Penny was just twenty-five when her husband of four years left her and their three-year-old daughter Molly for another woman. Penny confided in me often during those painful years, and I see real parallels with her and Leah.

Penny said, "I wanted Matt to be miserable with Brooke. I hoped she'd be bitchy and lazy and unresponsive in bed. I know that's terrible—but that's what I wanted. He had hurt us so badly—I wanted him to hurt too.

"When Molly would spend weekends with Matt and Brooke, I'd pump her for details. I know you are not supposed to do that to a child, but I did. I was so curious to see if my hopes were being fulfilled. One time Molly told me something that left me furious, humiliated, and heartbroken.

"Matt and Brooke had taken her camping. Apparently they thought she was asleep, because they made love with her next to them in the tent. Molly told me, 'I think Daddy was hurting Brooke because she kept moaning.'

"I called Matt and told him what I thought about his indiscreet behavior with Molly. He apologized profusely and I think he did feel badly. What he couldn't apologize for was loving Brooke more than he did me. I've cried buckets about that."

Leah must have cried buckets in her life. She had to watch Jacob's eyes light up when Rachel appeared; she had to watch him pull her sister tenderly to himself and whisper to her; and she had to sleep alone while Jacob was in the bedroom of her beautiful younger sister.

The Lord was compassionate toward Leah's plight: "When the Lord saw that Leah was not loved, he opened her womb, but Rachel was barren" (Genesis 29:31).

Leah spent years longing for her husband's love. She hoped that giving him sons would win his love. When she gave birth to her firstborn son, Reuben, she said, "Surely my husband will love me now'' (Genesis 29:32). She had three more sons, and each time hoped that this child would turn her husband's heart toward her. But it didn't.

Meanwhile, while four little boys clung to Leah's skirt, Rachel was barren. And Rachel was vexed by her sister's fertility.

## Rachel: the new wife

The new wife's life is not necessarily a bed of roses. When Ann Cryster interviewed second wives, she found many were insecure in their husband's love. For one thing, they knew he was capable of breaking his marriage vows. In addition, many saw evidence that he still had feelings of affection for his first wife. Cryster writes, ''Even though she [the new wife] has the license and the ring, she feels that the competition will never end. At the back of her mind lurks the fear that her husband still pines for his ex-wife, even more attractive now that she is forbidden fruit.''[4]

For Rachel, the competition lay in the fact that Leah was fertile and she was barren. Her older sister's sons surrounded her. The depth of Rachel's emotion is evident in her cry to Jacob: ''Give me children, or I'll die!'' (Genesis 30:1)

Jacob responded, ''Am I in the place of God, who has kept you from having children?'' (Genesis 30:2)

Rachel began bringing her maidservants to Jacob's bed in order to have children through them. She even named one of those sons ''Naphtali,'' which means ''My struggle,'' and said, ''I have had a great struggle with my sister, and I have won'' (Genesis 30:8). The focus of Rachel's life seemed to be her competition with Leah. A scene between Rachel and Leah shows me the torture that these two women inflicted on each other.

Leah's son Reuben found some valuable mandrake plants during a wheat harvest. Mandrakes were thought to make a woman fertile. Rachel humbled herself and went to Leah, saying, "Please give me some of you son's mandrakes" (Genesis 30:14).

Leah, realizing she had the upper hand, let her bitterness spew: "Wasn't it enough that you took away my husband? Will you take my son's mandrakes too?" (Genesis 30:15)

Rachel knew that Leah longed to sleep with Jacob, so she told Leah that, in exchange for the mandrakes, she would allow Jacob to sleep with her that night. How humiliating!

But Leah grabbed the chance and cried out to God to help her have another son. God listened to her and gave her a fifth and a sixth son. As with Rachel, the focus of Leah's life seemed to be her competition with her sister.

It is not unusual for competition with a "wife-in-law" to be a strong undercurrent in a woman's life. That rivalry escalates when there are children involved — and the children are the victims caught in the middle.

### The children
Bitterness, unfortunately, is the norm between wives-in-law. One study of the children of divorce found that only 14 percent said that their mother and stepmother were on good terms. Forty-five percent said the feelings ran high and negative![5]

Many first wives said it was hard for them to watch their ex-husband be a better father to his second set of children than he was to his first set. One woman told me, her green eyes flashing with anger, "Every year I remind both my ex and Sylvia that Kim's birthday is coming — but it doesn't do any good. He still forgets. It really rubs salt in Kim's wounds to see how attentive he is to the twins [his children by Sylvia]. As a teenager, Kim is acting out, I think, to get her dad's attention. She rolled her car last year and wound up in the hospital looking like she'd been beaten up by a gang. Could he come to see her? No — because the twins had Little League games every night that week. And I *HATE* Sylvia for not nudging him to be a decent father toward *all* his children."

## Peace despite pain

Amazingly, despite the great pain, some wives-in-law have made peace with one another. The women I have known who have succeeded in this most difficult of relationships are women who have matured in their walk with Christ. Ann Cryster says that the inability to forgive and the inability to conquer the debilitating emotions of jealousy, resentment, and bitterness are the two most common obstacles preventing a healthy relationship between wives-in-law. Cryster suggests seeking professional help — and I'd encourage looking for someone whose counsel will be based on the Word of God.

Leah struggled with resentment toward Rachel, in part, because of the favoritism Jacob showed toward Rachel's children. Jacob, a victim of parental favoritism and sibling rivalry himself, passed on this sin to his own children. He neglected Leah's children but lavished attention on Joseph, his son by Rachel, and later Benjamin, his other son by Rachel. Sibling rivalry ruled the home of Jacob.

> Now Israel [Jacob] loved Joseph more than any of his other sons, because he had been born to him in his old age; and he made a richly ornamented robe for him. When his brothers saw that their father loved him more than any of them, they hated him and could not speak a kind word to him (Genesis 37:3-4).

I have wondered whether Jacob's favoritism and the resulting sibling rivalry might have been curbed had Rachel and Leah found a way, in the Lord, to become friends. They could have presented a united front to Jacob and perhaps spared their children their painful rivalry. Though it seems a tremendous task, I believe it would have been possible, with God's help. But the indications are strong that Rachel and Leah's religion was cultural rather than spiritual. When Rachel left home, she stole her father's household gods! I suspect Rachel stole the idols because she believed they had power.

Personally, my relationship with Christ has helped me to be a better forgiver. When I think about *how much* I've been forgiven, it's harder to harbor unforgiveness in my heart. If Rachel had been a woman of faith, I believe she would have been able to forgive Leah for the part she played in Laban's deception. Instead, she held a grudge against Leah all of her life. Another evidence for her lack of faith is her conversation. Jesus says that what comes out of our mouth reveals what is in our hearts, and there are streams of unpleasantries from Rachel's mouth. Though Rachel was beautiful on the outside, she certainly wasn't a positive role model.

When unforgiveness abounds, children often lose respect for their parents. In her book, *Solomon's Children,* Glynnis Walker shares stories from adult children who viewed their parents' behavior as childish — and felt grieved that they were deprived of the joy that could have been theirs had their parents been able to behave maturely:

> They wouldn't attend the same family functions. Everyone had to phone around beforehand to make sure that so and so wasn't coming. If one showed up, the other left. My cousin's wedding was a fiasco. It made me very nervous about any sort of "family" occasion. So when I got married I didn't invite any of them, step-parents or parents, just some friends and my sister. I didn't want their stupidity to spoil my wedding.

> When my first child was born my mother and my stepmother both came to the hospital at the same time and went to the nursery to see the baby. My stepmother put her hand on my mother's arm to congratulate her. My mother reacted as if she had been touched by a leper and

> left the hospital building immediately. I felt sorry for my
> mother that she could be so hateful at such a joyous time.
> She missed so much she could have had.[6]

If a woman was able to behave in a reasonable fashion toward her wife-in-law, it impressed the children immeasur-
ably. One young woman said: "They were great friends. My
mother said she always liked Elaine and didn't blame her for
anything. It made me respect my mother an awful lot for
having such a mature attitude."[7]

In most cases, wives-in-law do encounter transgressions
to forgive. And they always suffer pain to be surmounted.
But they *can* done do it through the power we have in
Christl.

## The godly response of a wife-in-law

We can learn something of value from Leah's response to
her pain. After giving birth to five sons, and each time hoping, in vain, that her husband would love her, she *changed
dreams*. When she gave birth to her sixth son, she said:
"This time my husband will treat me with honor, because I
have borne him six sons" (Genesis 30:20). She was no longer
hoping for love, just respect. Commentator Larry Richards
says, "Life has meaning, even when hopes are unfulfilled."[8]

My friend Penny came to Christ after she married, but
her husband did not. Eventually he had an affair and left
her. For years, my friend Penny clung to the dream that
Matt would return to her and their little girl, Molly. She
said, "Even when the dream was chipped away at—by evi-
dences of Matt's contentment with Brooke [his new wife],
with the birth of their baby, and with their move to another
state—I still hoped.

"For years I clung unrealistically to the dream that Matt
would come back. In so doing, I hurt Molly. I fed *her* hope of
reconciliation. I did what I could to keep Molly from loving

Brooke, because I was afraid if she did, it would be another nail in the coffin of my marriage to Matt.

"But as time went by, God helped me to see I was robbing Molly of the joy of childhood – and possibly maiming her for life. One year, when she was just six, after she had spent Christmas with Matt and Brooke, I found her in her room in tears. She told me she hated Christmas. A six-year-old? Hating Christmas? As I drew her out, I heard her parroting my criticisms of Brooke. God convicted me that Molly was reflecting my bitterness – and out of loyalty to me, was withholding her love and cooperation. We had a long talk that night and I confessed to Molly that I had been wrong in not fully forgiving Brooke and her dad. That was a turning point. Her relationship with Matt and Brooke improved dramatically – and intriguingly, so did mine.

"I'm not sure Molly would be the godly young woman she is today if I had not grown up myself."

The first wife seems to find it easier to relinquish the dream of reconciliation if she remarries. (That's why so many second wives hope first wives will remarry!) But in Christ, a first wife can find peace without a husband. My friend Penny has – and other women have as well. Penny told me that she has found comfort in the story of Hagar.

"Hagar was a single mom like me. Abraham cast her out, along with his son, Ishmael, at Sarah's request. In the desert Hagar and Ishmael are sobbing when an angel of God calls out to her and says: 'What is the matter, Hagar? Do not be afraid; God has heard the boy crying as he lies there' (Genesis 21:17). We are also told that God was with Ishmael as he grew up. This passage has been a great comfort to me – and I have definitely seen evidence that God has seen our tears and that He has been with Molly as she has grown up."

Often this life *is* hard, but some wives-in-law make it even harder by dwelling on revenge. Ann Cryster found through her interviews that many women dreamed of wrecking their wife-in-law's car, stealing her clothes, or spying on her in aerobics class. Relinquishing the dream of revenge may feel like a sacrifice, but it yields a harvest of righteousness that can come in no other way. God cannot lead us down new paths if we have set our hearts on the old path. Our children are not likely to become godly individuals if their role models are harboring bitterness or dreams of revenge in their hearts. We reap what we sow. If we sow revenge, we will reap bitterness. If we sow love, we will reap joy. Ann Cryster makes a poignant plea:

> Will it really be such a bad thing if our daughter loves her stepmother? Will she really love us any less? In fact, what might make our kids appreciate us less is their sense of our compulsive competitiveness with their stepparents, because we tend at such times to be our worst selves. . . . It may feel like a frightening loss when our young daughter is delighted with her new stepmother, but, in fact, how can her added happiness detract from our own?[9]

The second wife also has pain to surmount and needs to draw upon her resources in Christ to do so. I spoke at a retreat in Los Angeles and stayed at the coordinator's home, who is a second wife. Kay's husband had come to Christ after his first marriage ended and then met and married Kay. For twenty years, Kay had been actively involved in the life of her stepdaughter, Lindy, though Lindy lived with her mother. Kay said, "Lindy is as precious to me as my biological daughters — and she spent lots of time with us. God has blessed us with a rare and special relationship." But Kay's relationship with her "wife-in-law" has been strained as JoAnne has brought repeated lawsuits against her ex-husband to keep him from seeing Lindy and for more support. When Lindy married this spring, Kay had fears about the visit to Green Bay for the impending wedding. "And my worst nightmares came true," she said. "If it hadn't been for the restraint the Lord gave me, I might have taken an early plane back and ruined Lindy's day."

Kay's wife-in-law invited Kay, her husband, and the bride-to-be for a whitefish dinner two nights before the wedding. Kay said, "JoAnne had been to the hairdresser in the morning and then had been drinking all day. I expected that there would be other guests — but it was just us. JoAnne's inhibitions were overcome by the liquor and she began reminiscing about her wedding to my husband. It was very, very hard. I also could see that Lindy still had hopes, despite the fact that Chuck and I have been married for twenty years, that her parents would reconcile."

The rehearsal showed Kay that the wedding was going to have its share of pain for her. Kay said, with her eyes welling with tears, "Three times during the ceremony Lindy's mother was honored — but not me. I watched my husband standing up with his beautiful daughter on his arm and respond to the question of 'Who gives this woman . . .' with 'Her mother and I do.' I was a mother to Lindy too — but I was completely unrecognized. I felt like the unwelcome guest, the persona non grata.

"The reception line was difficult too. It's a strange feeling to have your husband standing between you and his ex. We greeted 500 people and I felt God literally holding me up.

"But I am so thankful, looking back, for God's help. The morning of the wedding, I prayed that God would help me be gracious and to reflect Christ throughout the day. And though the sorrow was there, His grace prevailed. When everything was over Lindy's grandmother handed me a note that Lindy had written. Alone in my room, I read her precious thank-you for the part I'd played in her life."

Kay told me that when her children feel the pain of divorce, she often tells them, "This is why God hates divorce." If you are like Kay and are living with pain (and who of us isn't?) your pain doesn't need to be wasted. God can bring beauty out of ashes if you learn from your pain and then pass on what you've learned to younger women.

### In the next chapter . . .
In Titus 2, God asks "older women" to teach "younger women" to live in a way that is pleasing to Him. Sometimes we can help younger women avoid pain by encouraging them to make wise choices (marrying godly men, staying true to their marriage vows), and sometimes we can help younger women reduce pain by encouraging them to respond to difficulties in godly ways (forgiving, refusing to retaliate).

If you think you can't be a Titus 2 woman until you are forty, think again! For every woman is older than someone! I think you also will be amazed to discover what the word "teach" means in this famous passage. When I discovered the Greek meaning, the passage came alive with fresh insight!

# Bible Study for Individuals or Small Groups

Read the historical account, remembering the *Who? What? When? Why?* and *How?* questions.

Read Genesis 29:16-35 and make observations on 30-35.

Observations:

Principles to apply:

Application:

Read Genesis 30:1-22 and make observations on 8 and 15-22.

Observations:

Principles to apply:

Application:

Genesis 37:2-4


Observations:




Principles to apply:

Application:


Read Matthew 18:21-35. State the central point of the parable and record a personal application.


Observations:




Principles to apply:

Application:

*Likewise, teach the older women to be*
*reverent in the way they live,*
*not to be slanderers or addicted to much wine,*
*but to teach what is good. Then they can*
*train the younger women to love their husbands*
*and children, to be self-controlled and pure,*
*to be busy at home, to be kind,*
*and to be subject to their husbands,*
*so that no one will malign the word of God.*

Titus 2:3-5

ten
# Restoring Our Friends to Their Senses

"I can't even remember the last time Mike and I were intimate — that's how long it's been."

Amy's mug of coffee sat untouched, growing cold as she twisted her single blond braid, tearfully explaining the state of her sixteen-year marriage. "There's so much anger — we go to bed in icy silence. The only time we talk is when we exchange sarcastic barbs. Can you understand, Dee? I've got to get out of this marriage!" She searched my eyes for compassion.

I looked down. I knew Mike was a good man. Somehow Amy and Mike had gotten themselves into a downward spiral, but this wasn't a marriage that should end. I was afraid sympathy would push Amy over the divorce cliff, so I was quiet, trying to decide how to respond. The room was still.

My reserve infuriated Amy. She stood abruptly, grabbed her camel jacket from the back of the chair and said, "You don't understand! How easy it is for a happily married person to be self-righteous about divorce! Dee, you just don't know what it's like to live with a man you don't love any more. Mike never compliments me, never touches me. . . . Oh, never mind!"

Amy turned and headed for the door. I quickly followed, "Amy," I pleaded, catching her arm.

Jerking it away, she reached for the door: "I don't know why I came to you. I guess I was stupid enough to think that after eight years of friendship you might care about *my* pain." Sobbing, Amy ran to her car and screeched up the driveway.

Turning back into my house, I refuted her last accusation. I did care! I thought back to the night our friendship with Amy and Mike cemented. It had been Christmastime, and they and their three tow-headed tots had come caroling, offering a plate of fresh-from-the-oven sugar cookies: stars, bells, and snowmen dusted with sprinkles. We'd invited them in and talked and laughed for over an hour. Before they left I asked for an encore of "O Come All Ye Faithful" so I could take their picture. I pulled out the album and found it. How happy they looked! How could this family be ending? How could I make Amy think rationally?

The photo in my hand reminded me of a comment my friend Beth had made. Darkly attractive, with a rare mix of sophistication and warmth, Beth and her husband Dave had made a unique contribution to our adult Sunday School class. Both had been married before and vulnerably admit that leaving their first loves was a mistake, even though they are determined to make their marriage to each other work. I remember the day Beth stilled the class with her candor: "There's a million reasons not to leave your first love — right down to the little things — like photo albums! Who gets them? And who wants them? Because looking at your once-whole happy family is extremely painful."

I wondered if there was any chance that Amy might agree to meet with Beth. She'd been so angry when she left. If I called, would she cut me off, assuming I was getting ready to give her a sermon? How could I gain a hearing?

### Breaking down the barrier

I called Beth, explaining the situation with Amy and Mike. I told her that, though they were faithful church attenders, their church didn't emphasize personal faith or the Scriptures — so I wasn't sure how responsive she'd be to a scriptural approach.

Beth said: "I've found that even people who know Christ are not responsive to Scripture at this point. Often they've hardened their hearts because they feel God's way is too painful. The only thing that might work is to show them that divorce will be *more* painful. Amy needs to see what her life will be like if she divorces Mike. I'd be happy to meet with her!"

I so appreciated Beth's willingness — but I wondered, "Would Amy come?"

Sensing my thoughts, Beth said, "Dee, the fact that Amy came to you is a very hopeful sign. Let's bathe this situation in prayer. Then make a casserole, go over, and see if she's receptive."

Armed with lasagna, I rang Amy's doorbell. When she

opened the door and saw me, she softened. She took the pan from me and gestured for me to follow her into the kitchen. Placing it on the counter, she turned toward me tearfully and we embraced.

"I do care about you, Amy," I sobbed.

"I know," she gasped.

I told her about Beth, and then I said, "I promise — no pressure. I just thought talking to Beth would give you a better idea of what your life will be like if you divorce Mike."

Amy was quiet. Then she said, "I guess it couldn't hurt."

## Considering the consequences

We began talking while the October sun shone warmly through the window — and kept talking until it had sunk behind the golden trees on the hill across the lake.

Beth began, her voice intent. "I know you think, Amy, that it couldn't get any worse than it is. That divorce has to be better. But very very seldom does that turn out to be true. I'm absolutely convinced that God never intended us to leave our first loves, the spouse with whom we shared so many firsts: your children's births; Johnny's first steps; Mary's first dance when she floated down the steps into the living room; your first home; even those struggling first years when you existed on macaroni and cheese."

"Why did you leave your first love, Beth?" I asked while Amy listened silently, her cool hands finding comfort around the steaming mug of coffee.

Beth answered carefully: "Because I was deceived by my own heart — with a little help by the values all around me. I felt like life was passing me by. I began to be irritated by all kinds of little things about my husband. He was too skinny. I thought he had ugly fingers. He was a farmer and sometimes he had dirt in his ears. I know it sounds ridiculous, but at the time I felt that if there was going to be any hope for happiness for me, I had to leave.

"A few years after the divorce, though, I thought, 'What was the matter with me? He was a good man!' During that time of brokenness I came to Christ. But though He made me a new creation, and filled the emptiness in me, that doesn't mean I escaped the consequences of my sinful choice."

I got up and filled our coffee cups. "Tell us about those consequences," I prodded.

"It's hard to know where to start. There are big things, of course, but almost harder are the daily little tensions. Like how you'll feel at your child's basketball game as he looks longingly back and forth between you and your ex, who has carefully placed himself on the opposite end of the bleachers.

"There's the endless tension about money. Even now with our kids grown, who pays for school books, graduation expenses, the wedding reception? You may think things are tight now—but you'll probably become one of America's new poverty class: the single mother. Ask around, Amy, and see how divorcees are living.

"But the worst pain is that we've permanently damaged our children. We let them down. Their role models betrayed their trust and they are in search of different role models. Their chances of a happy marriage have been drastically re-duced—the statistics verify that. And we feel a lack of re-spect. Sometimes they openly verbalize it. It hurts, Amy."

Beth took out a tissue and blew her nose loudly. We laughed, relieving our tension. I said, "I think it's time for food!" We laughed again, glad for a momentary diversion. I brought out cheese, apples, and knives. I put a bowl of fresh-ly toasted pumpkin seeds on the table.

Reaching for a handful, Beth said, reflectively, "Family traditions, like carving pumpkins and putting up the Christ-mas tree, are changed. The kids are always thinking of the missing parent. We all dread the holidays. The kids aren't eager to be with me or my ex-husband. They aren't particularly comfortable with our new spouses. Home isn't home. There's constant friction concerning where they'll go, and when they come it's painful — because it isn't the same for them. It isn't the same for me either. I can't turn to David and say, 'Do you remember the Christmas when Johnny . . .' because David wasn't there. And special occasions, like birthdays, graduations, weddings, etc., are all filled with distress. The pain won't quit — and often, it's terribly intense."

"How old were your children when you left?" Amy asked.

Beth smiled, seeming to read her thoughts. "Only one was still in the nest — and she was in her senior year so she stayed with my husband. Lots of people will tell you that once the kids are out of the nest, it's OK to leave, but I'll tell you, Amy, it's not so. My oldest daughter, who was twenty-four, suffered the most. I repeat: We've permanently damaged our children. Their self-esteem. Their security. Their memories. Their future. And, even though they are grown now, the pain continues. Our relationship with our grandchildren, for example, is extremely complicated. They've got so many grandparents, they're not even sure what to call us all!"

Beth shook her head sadly: "Humpty Dumpty cannot be put back together again — at least not in this world. The sins of the fathers, and the mothers, are visited on the next generation, and the next, and the next."

Amy was silent. Thoughtful. Beth interrupted her pensiveness with a question. "Amy, have you told the children what you're considering?"

Twisting her braid, Amy responded, "I've talked to the two older ones. I wanted to know, if they had a choice, with whom they would live. Our son said he didn't know. And our daughter said she would leave it up to the judge because she didn't want to hurt either of our feelings. I'd been so confident they'd both choose me. Now I'm not sure."

"It puts them in a terrible position," Beth responded. "And they'll hate you for doing it to them. I have another question, Amy. It's none of my business, but I'm going to ask anyhow. Is there someone else?"

I was shocked to see Amy nod. But Beth seemed to expect it.

Amy glanced at me and said, "There's been nothing physical. But there's a man at work who makes me feel good about myself. In a way that Mike hasn't for a long, long time."

"Satan knows when to attack," Beth said. "Amy, you have to separate yourself from this man. Satan is waiting at the door, longing to overpower you. He seeks to destroy you and your family." Beth continued. "If you divorce Mike, Amy, how will you feel when he finds someone else?"

Amy said, "I've been telling myself no one else would want him."

"Amy!" I interrupted. "Mike is kind and hard-working! Beth, let me show you his picture." I got out the album and started looking.

As I turned pages, Beth said, "Even if he's homely, Amy, women will flock around him. He'll be remarried within two years. Count on it. And chances are, he'll marry a divorcee with kids. Kids with whom your kids will have to share their dad and their lives."

I showed Beth the picture of the family, singing a carol on our front porch. Mike, a good-looking, muscular man, had his arm around Amy, his blue eyes full of joy.

"Wow," Beth breathed, shaking her head.

Amy took the picture from Beth, looking at Mike, as if with new eyes. She admitted, "When I think of Mike with someone else, I realize I still have some feelings. I've felt like if the divorce didn't work, I could have Mike back. But maybe not."

At this encouragement, Beth leaned over and put her hand on Amy's. "I'm convinced it's possible to restore the feelings you and Mike had for each other in the beginning. If you start, Amy, I'm confident you have the power to release Mike's love for you. Men long for respect from their wives. When Mike feels that again, you'll see a change in his attitude toward you. I've counseled other women who felt like you did—and I've seen them, because of a change of attitude, and with help from God, turn their marriage back to what it was in the beginning."

Amy turned a corner that day. She left with a different perspective. That night she fixed Mike's favorite supper: stuffed pork chops. She put candles on the table. The next day when Amy told me about it, she seemed lighter, freer. She laughed when she told me, "Mike walked in the door, saw the candles, and said, angrily: 'Who's coming for dinner?' He looked so surprised when I told him it was just for him and the kids."

Amy took another important step when she confronted the man at work who'd been unusually attentive toward her. She called Beth and said, "I told him some of the things you told me. And I told him, in no uncertain terms, that I was recommitting myself to my marriage. He's backed off gracefully."

God wants women to "train," or teach, younger women in the Christian lifestyle (Titus 2:4-5). The word *train* is from a Greek word meaning "to restore to one's senses, to make sound of mind, to hold one to his duty." My friend Beth taught me a lot, through her example, about how to bring younger women "to their senses." The hardline approach of shooting Scripture at them often backfires, but if you can help them to see that the consequences of their choice (whether it is divorce, infidelity, abortion, or something else destructive) could be very painful, you may gain a listening ear.

I have also learned, however, that if a woman doesn't know Christ, you are at best treating symptoms. You must get to the decaying root. Amy and Mike slowly rekindled their marriage, and for the next year, they seemed to be on the road to recovery. Then, like a rollar coaster, they plummeted to the bottom. Right now things look hopeful again. But I have come to realize that, though God allowed Beth and me to steer Amy back on track, her recovery, without Christ, is probably going to be only temporary.

I realized this again recently after talking to a young woman on an airplane, trying to encourage her, as Titus 2 instructs, "to love her children." Pregnant with her first child, she told me she was going to put him in day care at six weeks. As I drew her out with questions, it became apparent that it wasn't financial necessity, but a choice. I shared with her, as I had seen Beth do with my friend Amy, what the consequences of her choice could be. Connie Marshner's book, *Can Motherhood Survive?* has some riveting information on the differences between children reared by their mothers and those reared by sitters, daycares, and relatives. I felt she was "coming to her senses" and thinking carefully about my words. But I also left thinking that, unless this young woman came to Christ, it was going to be very hard for her to stay sane, to hold to her duty, and to resist the rising tides of our times.

### Bringing women to Christ

Often those who are most passionate about bringing others to Christ are new Christians. When I was a new Christian, I practically stopped people in the grocery store. I left tracts everywhere. I was constantly aware of the fact that they might be headed toward eternity without a Savior. But as the years went by, I lost that zeal. I transferred some of it toward social issues, like abortion and pornography. And while I believe those *are* important, and that part of being

salt and light means trying to slow down the decadence in
our world, God has reminded me that my most important
mission is to bring others to Him. God has used a friend to
renew my vision. Marilyn Pendleton, a winsome young
mother of three with a 600-watt smile, has a very aggressive
form of cancer, and her doctors give her little hope. But her
attitude is amazing. She wrote to me, saying, "Two years
ago I realized I'd lost my passion, my first love, and I told
God to do whatever it took to restore it. Although many
have viewed this as a tragedy, it has been a gift. Not many
people get a picture of their own mortality at age thirty-six.
God has given me a new urgency, a new boldness, about
sharing Christ."

Marilyn has caused me to search my own heart: Have I
lost my first love? My urgency? My boldness for sharing
Christ?

God has also shown me that the *only* way we can see lasting fruit in peoples' lives is through the conversion of their
hearts. Knowing Christ does make a difference! When I sur-
veyed women in order to write my book *The Lifestyles of
Christian Women,* I found that women who truly know Him
*are* living differently. These women are much less likely to
divorce, to abort their children, or to be apathetic about how
those children are raised. The way we can be *most* effective
as Titus 2 women is through evangelism and discipleship.

If you have lost your compassion for the lost, ask Jesus to
touch your eyes for a second time, so that you see people,
"not as trees walking," but as people who are running toward the precipice of hell. As Paul says so eloquently,
"Since, then, we know what it is to fear the Lord, we try to
persuade men" (2 Corinthians 5:11).

Women, who tend to have strong friendships, have a myriad of opportunities for personal evangelism — whether it's
through small group Bible study, or one-on-one sharing, or
an invitation to an evangelistic event. But unless you care,

you won't be used of the Lord. I agree with the late Paul Little, who said that he never knew anyone effective in personal evangelism who didn't have an attitude of compassion and expectancy toward each person he or she met.[1]

**In the next chapter . . .**
I am not saying that once a young woman knows Christ — ZAP — all is well, all is easy. The Christian life is a difficult sojourn, and we need to continually be reaching out to one another, helping one another up, like mountain climbers determined to reach the top. One of the most challenging trails we have to follow is that of motherhood, and, too often, we determine to climb to the top alone. I know I have personally been in the situation where I am in desperate need of a hand, like a mountain climber who has lost her footing, and yet I am hesitant to ask my friends for help.

# Bible Study for Individuals or Small Groups

Look for commands, comparisons, and key phrases and words.

Titus 2:3-5

Observations:

Meaning:

Application:

1 Timothy 5:9-10

Observations:

Meaning:

Application:

# Restoring Our Friends to Their Senses

2 Corinthians 5:11, 14-21

Observations:

Meaning:

Application:

Revelation 2:4-5

Observations:

Meaning:

Application:

# eleven

# When You're Hesitant to Ask for Help

"I can't be sick, Lord!"

Nauseated, I fell back on the pillow and continued pleading. "Please, Lord — not with two ever-present toddlers!"

I pulled my legs into a fetal position and waited for instant healing.

"Plan B. Please, Lord, if I have to be sick, at least let the boys sleep in this morning."

No sooner had I uttered my prayer than I heard the squeak of the crib rail from the nursery and the soft thump of little feet, clad in Winnie-the-Pooh pajama sleepers, hitting the floor. I shut my eyes against the inevitable. The bedroom door burst open. The smell of soggy diaper filled the air as Johnny stood beside my bed, watching me. Discerning my sleep was feigned, he said, "Mommy, I'm hungry."

"Mommy's sick, Sweetheart. Do you think you could find the Pop Tarts in the cupboard? And could you bring me a diaper?"

He padded quickly away. I hoped his assignment would take a long, long time.

But in two minutes he was back, Pop Tart in hand. Dropping crumbs, Johnny crawled first on the bed, then on me. Small, sticky fingers pried open my eyelids. "Are you better yet, Mommy?"

I considered calling Patti. I knew she would take the boys, but I didn't want to impose. Patti was important to me — what if my request strained our friendship? I didn't call.

Before that incredibly long day was over, J.R., our first-born, downed a whole bottle of orange-flavored children's aspirin as his inattentive mother dozed on the couch. We emptied his stomach and he survived, but I began to see my foolishness in not calling Patti.

That day occurred twenty-five years ago and those toddlers are now men. Our three daughters are all in school, so when I get sick, I sleep in uninterrupted bliss. But if I really need help, I've learned to ask.

Asking for help, rather than being a sign of weakness, is a sign of strength because it demonstrates humility, the recognition that there are times in my life when I need help to carry an over-burden. And if the need is genuine, rather than straining a friendship, asking for help cements it.

## Cementing a friendship

Early on in my friendship with Shell, I found myself in need again. I was scheduled to speak at a luncheon in Lincoln. The only child we had at home at that time was Sally. My plan was to drop her at school and then get on I-80 and head for my speaking engagement. On the way to school, however, Sally vomited in the front seat. We made a hasty retreat for home, where I cleaned up my daughter, put her in bed, and went back to clean up the car and, finally, myself. With time getting short, I was frantically trying to come up with solutions. As I cleaned, I thought of three options:

#1    I could call and cancel. ("But how can I, Lord? They're expecting 300 women! They've been planning for months!")

#2    I could take Sally with me and have her lie down in the coat room. (I pictured my little waif huddled behind the coats with a bucket while I spoke about being a good mother.)

#3    I could call Shell, who was my closest friend in this new town, and ask for help. ("But isn't this a lot to ask, Lord? Is our friendship too young?")

The third option, though frightening to me, seemed the best. Hesitantly, I picked up the phone. I explained my dilemma to Shell – and then I gave her room to squiggle out if she felt imposed upon. I said, "If you have something else going on today, that's fine, because I have other options." And then I prayed and held my breath, hoping I wouldn't have to use one of those other very undesirable options.

Without hesitation, Shell said: "Bring her right over. I insist. I'm getting a bed ready."

Shell's enthusiastic response lifted the burden from my

shoulders. Had she said, "Well, if you can't find someone else . . ." I would have retreated. I might even have felt "let down," despite the fact I had minimized my need. How I pray that I can be as intuitive and flexible as Shell was when a woman comes to me and drops clues about a deep need!

Sally brightened to see the room Shell had prepared. Blue-flowered pillows had been fluffed against the headboard of the bed. A stack of comic books, a hand-held video game, and a tall glass of 7-Up sat on the bedside table.

No longer reluctant to have me leave, Sally hugged me good-bye. Feeling considerably lighter, I walked down the stairs with Shell. Before I left, we paused for a moment to pray. It touched me deeply when Shell said with emotion, "Thank You so much, dear Lord, that Dee trusted me enough to come to me with her need."

**Hearing the unspoken request**
I have found linguist Deborah Tannen's observations about the way women make requests fascinating. Tannen says we are much less direct than men because we are more concerned about "breaking connections." Rather than saying, "Could you take care of Tommy tomorrow while I go to the dentist?" many women will instead hint, saying, "I don't know what to do with Tommy while I'm at the dentist tomorrow." Now any dodo bird should know she's asking for help with Tommy, but she doesn't dare to be direct. This teaches me to read between the lines when a soulmate shares a need with me — and to respond enthusiastically with an offer to help.

A woman named Julie Hines wrote me a particularly moving story of a time in her life when she desperately needed her friend, Suzanne — but was afraid to ask.

Julie wrote, "When my husband and I were overseas, we faced the greatest crisis of our lives when our baby was born with spina bifida. Even though my husband was wonderful,

I needed a woman friend to help carry my pain. I needed Suzanne. Without my having to ask, because I couldn't ask for so much, she moved a little of heaven and earth to fly over. I will never forget our greeting scene in the Bologna airport. It felt like a physical lightening of my load."

## When you need advice

Many times in my walk as a Christian wife and mother, I've needed advice. It's not nearly as hard to ask for advice as it is for other kinds of help. Perhaps as a result, often my first response when I'm troubled is to pick up the phone and call an empathetic friend. But God has been teaching me that a woman who is mature will run first to Him. Until I have been still before Him, until I have sought the Scriptures for His wisdom, it's too soon to run to a friend.

When we were living in Seattle, I was trying to teach our new springer spaniel puppy, "Darling," to stay within the boundaries of our yard without a fence. While reading on our back porch one autumn afternoon, I heard the angry cries of my neighbor. "GET OUT! SCAT! YOU *$#*+&*#* DOG!!!!!!" I looked up, alarmed, to see Darling digging in her rhododendrons.

I ran over, scooped up our puppy, and said, "I'm so sorry!"

My neighbor stormed into her house, slamming the door behind her. I retreated up our path with Darling. I asked myself, "What could I do to smooth this over?" My husband often received fish from his patients. So I went to our freezer, took out a salmon, and headed back to my neighbor's. When she opened the door, I said, "Would you take this salmon as a peace offering?"

She surprised me by saying: "Fish! I've got a freezer full of fish! That's the last thing I need." Then she closed the door in my face.

Embarrassed, I retreated again. In the safety of my house,

I curled up in an overstuffed chair and nursed my wounds, telling the Lord that I *had* tried. After all, Darling was just a puppy — wasn't my neighbor partly to blame for being so intolerant? And I *had* apologized — wasn't my neighbor now the one who was in the wrong? Wasn't the ball in *her* court?

My first response was to call a friend whom I knew would empathize with me — who would tell me how honorably I'd behaved and what a rat my neighbor was. I called Patti — no answer. Beth — her line was busy. Lorinda — nobody home. Beth — still busy.

Forced to go to the Friend who wasn't busy and was at home, I sat down and prayed again: "Lord, what should I do now?"

Instead of comforting me, He brought Romans 12:18 to mind: "If it is possible, as far as it depends on you, live at peace with everyone."

It seemed the Lord was nudging me to try again! Reluctantly, I looked around. Our flowers were past their bloom. Our cookie jar, empty.

"Lord," I said, "I don't have anything to give her!"

I am convinced that our Lord has a great sense of humor, for at that moment, the UPS truck pulled up in front. The man carried a crate of beautiful Florida oranges and grapefruit to our door — a gift from my mother-in-law. Moments later I was headed back to my neighbor's with a cardboard tray of citrus fruit. After ringing the doorbell, I stood there, nervously. This time, when she opened the door, she was the astonished one. After a long silence, she broke into a grin. "You don't give up, do you, honey?" She took the fruit and walked away, shaking her head and chuckling.

I learned so much from this experience, for my relationship with that neighbor was warm and good from that moment on. Whereas she hadn't been particularly friendly before, now she smiled and waved when I drove into the driveway. If I had been successful in reaching a friend when

I needed advice, she probably would have sympathized with me, telling me I had tried hard enough. That's not to say that friends always give poor advice, but simply to say that the very best advice, the advice that can never be wrong, is from the Lord.

If you've gone to the Lord and He seems silent and the way seems unclear, I believe it's appropriate to go to a woman friend. But go to the godliest women you know — particularly women who have been where you are going and have done it well.

**In the next chapter . . .**
Not too long ago my husband and I went to the Lord for His advice. God spoke to my husband, impressing on his heart that we should adopt an older, handicapped child. But when I prayed, I didn't hear anything. I only felt FEAR! If you were me, what would you have done?

# Bible Study for Individuals or Small Groups

Proverbs 15:12 and 15:22

Observations:

Meaning:

Application:

Proverbs 15:31-33

Observations:

Meaning:

Application:

# And Then We Were Women

Proverbs 16:21-25

Observations:

Meaning:

Application:

Esther 4:6-17 (If you are unfamiliar with the story of Esther, read it! In this passage, why are Esther and Mordecai direct? Look for other observations and principles in this narrative passage.)

Observations:

Principles to apply:

Application:

*We are not meant to remain as children*
*at the mercy of every chance wind....*
*But we are meant to hold firmly*
*to the truth in love, and to grow up*
*in every way into Christ, the Head.*

Ephesians 4:14-15 (PH)

twelve
# Growing Up into Christ the Head

God compares spiritual maturity to a mature human body, with individual believers as parts of the body and Christ as the head. Repeatedly God stresses that every part of the body is important and that "there should be no division in the body, but that its parts should have equal concern for each other" (1 Corinthians 12:25).

This analogy is particularly meaningful to us as women, for relationships are the most important part of our lives. Those relationships are not intended to conflict; rather, God intends for those relationships (with Him, with family, with friends) to work together in a harmonious whole, supporting each other. That is possible, however, only "if we do not remain as children" but "grow up in every way into Christ, the Head." I'd like to close this book with a personal story that illustrates this truth beautifully.

When Steve and I prayed about adopting again, he had the impression that he heard a young girl crying. When he told me this, I was overcome with fear. My life was jam-packed with our four children, my writing, and a heavy speaking schedule. How could I be a good mother to another child, especially, an older, handicapped child? Steve didn't pressure me but suggested we see if the Lord confirmed this leading in other ways.

A few days later I received a call from Barbara Kim, the caseworker at Holt, the Christian adoption agency through whom we had adopted our daughter Anne.

Innocently, Barbara said, "Would you consider adopting a ten-year-old girl from an orphanage in Thailand? All that's wrong with her is that she's missing her left arm. It was amputated and she was abandoned as a baby. But she's a survivor! She has such an uplifting spirit — like your Sally. She's just a year older than your Annie, so she'd fit perfectly in your family! Could I send you her picture?"

When Steve saw Beth's picture, he was ready to go to Thailand! But he told me, genuinely, that we wouldn't do it unless God gave *me* a peace about it as well.

But peace seemed nowhere near! I felt like God was asking me to sail into a storm! Like a rowboat on the high seas, I tossed about, wanting to be supportive of my husband, but overcome with fears. I *had* prayed, but the way seemed dark and cloudy. At that point it seemed wise to seek godly counsel, so I sought out spiritually mature women who would do their best to help me discern God's will.

And each of these women spoke to me truly, because they are growing up into Christ, the Head.

### Shell Ramey: earnest counsel

Shell listened to me intently, the way I knew she would. She prayed with me – and then she went home. She spent the whole day in prayer and in Scripture. Then she wrote me a ten-page letter. First she wrote out many Scriptures that she thought might be helpful to me – Scriptures like the following:

> Religion that God our Father accepts as pure and faultless is this: to look after orphans and widows in their distress.
> (James 1:27)

> Wives, submit to your husbands as to the Lord. For the husband is the head of the wife as Christ is the head of the church, His body, of which He is the Savior. Now, as the church submits to Christ, so also wives should submit to their husbands in everything.
> (Ephesians 5:22-24)

Then, to soften the blow of the Scriptures, she wrote me a beautiful, loving letter, telling me that it seemed to her that the Lord was leading us to do this, but that if I didn't receive His peace, that she didn't think I should go ahead. Either way, she would stand by my side.

### Jean Hueser: praying with me for wisdom

I walk with my friend Jean regularly, and it is our habit to walk and talk, then walk and pray. During this time of indecision, Jean prayed with me every day, pleading with God for His guidance. One prayer of Jean's which I remember was, "Lord, please put Your desires in Dee's heart. Give her Your peace if this is of You."

## Sara Andreesen: drawing out the deep waters of my soul

Solomon says, "The purposes of a man's heart are deep waters, but a man of understanding draws them out" (Proverbs 20:5). So, over taco salads at a restaurant appropriately called Amigos, Sara drew me out. This was our conversation, as I recall it.

"Dee," Sara began, "let's try to figure out why you are afraid. Are you afraid because this girl is ten years old? Are you afraid it's too late to mold her?"

"A little," I responded. "Many children don't survive being raised in an institution — they are emotionally maimed and can't seem to recover. But the social workers seem so confident that she's a survivor. And, at forty-eight, I wouldn't want a baby — or even a toddler. In fact, I *like* it that she's close in age to Annie. Perhaps God has this planned, in part, for Annie."

"Well, then," Sara continued. "Let's see. Are you afraid of her handicap? Are you afraid there are many things she won't be able to do and that you will constantly be helping her?"

"I don't think so." I answered. "Steve works with amputees a lot and he thinks that since she's been without her arm all her life, that there's very little she won't be able to do." I paused, emotion rising in me.

"Go on," Sara encouraged.

"He says she will probably do some things with her teeth and her feet."

"And how do you feel about that?" Sara prodded.

Now my tears were flowing. "I don't want her to do things with her teeth and her feet."

Sara sipped her coke. She had drawn out the deep waters of my soul. What we found wasn't very pretty: I was worried about appearances! Then she reached over and clasped my hand, laughing softly, empathetically. "You are mature in so many ways, Dee," she began gently, "but maybe this is an area where God is asking you to grow."

Solomon says, "Wounds from a friend can be trusted" (Proverbs 27:6).

### Janet Yost: an offer to stand by my side and help

Finally, I went to my friend Janet. Janet is a godly older woman — she is where I want to be in ten years. She is *so* patient and loving as she ministers to those in need, particularly those from other countries who are lonely, poor, and struggling to learn English.

Like my other friends, Janet told me that she felt I should have God's peace before I went ahead. But then she said, "If you do this, Dee, I will stand by your side and help you. You can bring your daughter to my house for an hour every day, and I will help her to learn English."

The writer of Ecclesiastes says, "Two are better than one, because they have a good return for their work: If one falls down, his friend can help him up. But pity the man who falls and has no one to help him up!" (Ecclesiastes 4:9-10)

The cumulative effect of my multitude of counselors was that God filled me with His peace, the sign for which everyone had been praying!

### Stepping out in faith

Steve, Sally, and I flew to Bangkok to meet Beth. We will never forget that adventure of faith! I saw confirmation upon confirmation that my sisters in Christ had worked together with God to help me find His plan for our family.

When the agency originally called, they asked us to fly to Bangkok on February 1 and return two weeks later with our new daughter. I went upstairs and looked at my calendar: in that two week period I had retreats in California, Kansas, and Rhode Island. I realized that, because I had given my word to those retreat committees years earlier, now I couldn't go and get my daughter. Steve and Sally would have to go without me.

My peace evaporated. It seemed like I wasn't going to be getting off to a very good start as Beth's mother.

Yet, as my faith was flagging, women in the body of Christ took up the slack. The Kansas retreat committee began praying, in earnest, that the authorities in Thailand would change their mind and postpone our trip for two weeks. (Beginning February 14, I was free until the end of the month.)

Shortly before Steve and Sally were to leave without me, Cheri, a worker from the agency called and said, "We're sorry to tell you this, but your trip has been postponed until February 14." I surprised her with a shout of joy!

I am *so thankful* I was able to go. I will never forget the greeting scene with our new daughter. How overjoyed she was to have a mother, a father, *a family*. How excited she was about the little things that you and I take for granted: Beds! Showers! Pizza! From the day we met Beth until today she has been a joyful child — filling our own hearts with her overflow. While we were in Thailand we took a trip to the beach, where I took this picture of our new daughter.

*Beth in Thailand*

But the most amazing confirmation came from a social worker in Thailand. After a few days with our cheerful daughter, I asked, "When my husband and I prayed about adopting Beth, he heard a girl crying. Beth had just had her tenth birthday. What was happening in her life then?"

The social worker responded immediately: "She gave up hope. Knowing we rarely find a home for a child over ten, she thought she would never have a mother or a father, and she began to sink into a depression. She was weepy, withdrawn. . . . But shortly after that we received the news that a home *had* been found. And her joy returned!"

I do not know why God, out of all of the thousands of orphans who need homes, responded to *Beth's* cry. I doubt that I will know that until I see Christ face-to-face. But I do know that I would not have had the courage to step out in faith were it not for the wisdom and support my sisters in Christ gave to me.

Our journey with Beth *is* stretching me, as my friend Sara predicted. Yet as so often happens, my greatest worry has turned out to be nothing. Beth is so skilled that most people forget, after being with her for a while, that she's missing an arm. Of course I've managed to find some new things to worry about — but as I am growing up into Christ the Head, I am learning to cast those anxieties on Him.

The other night at supper Beth wanted to lead us in a cheer. Steve and I had tears in our eyes as we cooperated with her lead:

      Beth:  Give me an F!
    Family:  F!
      Beth:  Give me an A!
    Family:  A!
      Beth:  Give me an M!
    Family:  M!
      Beth:  Give me an I!
    Family:  I!

       Beth:   Give me an L!
    Family:   L!
       Beth:   Give me a Y!
    Family:   Y!
       Beth:   What do I have?
    Family:   FAMILY!

## Growing up in every way into Christ, the Head

God has ordained the family, and He has ordained fellowship among the believers. The Scriptures are full of portraits of each. They can work together in a beautiful harmonious whole as they flow from Christ, the Head. And so I
close this book with a prayer for you, my reader, and now my
friend:

> *Father, I pray that the woman who is reading this book
> will grow in You, becoming healthy and mature, and in so
> doing, be strengthened to help others: mothers, daughters,
> sisters, friends, and others in her life, so that they too may
> grow up into Christ the Head.*
>
> *I praise You, Father, that You are mindful of her, that You
> are a God who hears a child crying, a God who leans down
> and answers our prayers.*
>
> *I ask this in the name of Christ, our Intercessor.*

# Bible Study for Individuals or Small Groups

Look for commands, comparisons, and key phrases and words.

Proverbs 27:6

Observations:

Meaning:

Application:

Proverbs 27:9

Observations:

Meaning:

Application:

Proverbs 20:5

Observations:


Meaning:

Application:

Ecclesiastes 4:10

Observations:


Meaning:

Application:

Read Ephesians 4:11-16 and make observations on verses 13 through 15.

Observations:


Meaning:

Application:

Take time with these questions, recording your answers on a separate page, or in your journal.

1.  Describe the transformation that should take place in us according to 1 Corinthians 13:11.

2.  According to the text of *And Then We Were Women*, contrast the behavior and thinking of girls and young sisters with that of mature women. List several examples.

3.  In which of the above areas do you feel challenged to grow?

4.  Describe immature behavior as you saw it in the lives of Leah and Rachel.

5.  Describe mature behavior as you saw it in the lives of Mary and Elizabeth.

6.  Describe mature mothering as you saw it in the life of Jochebed.

7.  What from the above scriptural models is impacting you personally? Why?

8.  Describe mature love according to 1 Corinthians 13:4-7, illustrating it with three illustrations from *And Then We Were Women*.

9.  Now illustrate mature love with three recent examples from your own life or the life of a friend.

10. Describe the concept of marriage work, illustrating it from the Song of Songs or the friendship of Mary and Elizabeth.

11. How are you applying the concept of marriage work to your life?

12. What are some things you learned about older women teaching younger women — restoring them to their senses, mentoring them, and mothering them? How are you applying this concept personally?

13. What did you learn about how to study Scripture?

14. What lasting impact do you expect this study to have on your life? Be specific.

# Bible Study Notes

## SAMPLE OBSERVATIONS ON A DIDACTIC PASSAGE

Here are some of my notes from personal Bible study. Note how it helps to continually ask questions, examining every word, comparison, contrast, and order before turning to outside helps.

**Proverbs 14:1:** "The wise woman builds her house, but with her own hands the foolish one tears hers down."

### Personal observations
Comparison:
  Wise woman *builds,* foolish woman *tears down.*
Order:
  "With her own hands" *begins* the phrase, giving it emphasis.
Words:
  *her* — implies woman's ownership, responsibility, power.
  *builds* — implies effort, forethought.
  *house* — could mean actual house, furnishings. Could also mean people in it. I think context leans toward the latter.
Phrases:
  *tears down* — You could destroy the actual house through neglect, or through poor money management. You could destroy a marriage through neglect, infidelity, nagging. You could destroy children through neglect, harshness, permissiveness.

### Additional observations with the help of study aids
Other translations:
  The *King James Version* uses the word *plucketh* instead of *tears down.* This implies a gradual "nitpicking." Reminds me of nagging.
*Strong's Concordance* (Hebrew meanings of words):
  *tears down* from "harac" meaning to tear down, break down, beat down, destroy utterly
  *builds* from "banah" meaning to build, cause to continue
  *house* from "bayith" meaning especially family but also the dwelling place: winter house, palace, prison, temple

Cross-references:

Proverbs 31: Godly wife brings her husband good, not harm, all the days of his life and her children rise up and call her blessed.

Commentaries:

*Bible Knowledge Commentary:* A wise woman cares for the people in her home, helping them to flourish.

*Matthew Henry:* This was interesting because he came almost completely from the perspective of the physical house, seeing in this verse a foolish wife who squandered money and didn't keep the house neat and clean!

*Adam Clarke:* Likewise — a foolish wife is one who is thriftless and has dilapidated furniture!

## Meaning

The woman in the home impacts the family enormously. Through careful planning, diligence, and persistence she can make an eternal difference in the lives of family members. Through carelessness she can destroy them.

## Personal application

I need to plan how to build up my husband and children by putting effort into the supper conversation and atmosphere as well as the meal. This week I'll encourage discussing a proverb each night as well as sharing things we are thankful for in each other.

## SAMPLE OBSERVATIONS ON A NARRATIVE PASSAGE

**Luke 1:36-38:** " 'Even Elizabeth your relative is going to have a child in her old age, and she who was said to be barren is in her sixth month. For nothing is impossible with God.'

" 'I am the Lord's servant,' Mary answered. 'May it be to me as you have said.' Then the angel left her."

### Observations

Use the *Who? Where? When? What? How?* and *Why?* questions to probe this narrative passage. Often, to get the answers, one must look at the surrounding context as well. Sometimes these questions yield obvious observations, but often one will open the door to great insight — and you suddenly realize why God has seen fit to give you the historical details He did. Don't be afraid to ask questions for which you do not have answers!

● *Who?* Gabriel is talking to Mary about her cousin Elizabeth. The child Elizabeth will bear is *John the Baptist,* the forerunner of Jesus.

● *Where?* Mary is in *Nazareth.* Elizabeth, whom she will shortly visit, is about *100 miles away,* outside of *Jerusalem.* A long walk or donkey ride!

● *When?* Elizabeth is six months pregnant when Mary gets the news. Mary stayed with her three months. Did she stay for the birth of John? If so, was that to help prepare Mary for giving birth without a midwife?

● *What?* Gabriel's message is that nothing is impossible with God! Mary's response is "I am the Lord's servant."

● *How?* How was Mary feeling? We know she had been troubled (verse 29) but now seems accepting. The news about Elizabeth helped. Perhaps because she knew she wasn't the only one experiencing a miraculous pregnancy. She knew she'd have a friend who'd believe and support her. Perhaps because she was reminded of God's power. Her response of faith was fast — in contrast to Zechariah's.

● *Why?* Why did Gabriel tell Mary about Elizabeth? Perhaps because God knew Mary would need a friend, a mentor. Perhaps to encourage her faith. Perhaps because God knew Elizabeth needed Mary as a friend. Why did Mary respond with such trust? She was a remarkable woman. Perhaps her trust and faith is what caused her to find favor with God.

**Principles to apply**

In a narrative passage, look for principles. It's dangerous to skip this step, because God works with various people in various ways. For example, we won't all go to heaven in a chariot as Elijah did, nor will we experience a miraculous pregnancy, as Mary did. But still, all Scripture is profitable because we learn principles which can be applied to us.

Some principles I see are: nothing is impossible with God; submissiveness to God's plan is a commendable model; and, though God's plan may involve difficulties, He will also be with you, guiding you and caring for you.

**Application**

We've recently adopted an older child from Thailand, and this adjustment time can be difficult. But I need to trust, as Mary did, and realize that God's leading doesn't eliminate difficulties along the way. God surely led Mary to be the mother of Jesus — but the road was hard. And yet it can be filled with the joy and excitement of being on *God's* journey. Seeing how God provided for Mary by giving her encouragement and a mentor like Elizabeth reminds me of God's care for us and helps me to respond in trust as Mary did.

# Endnotes

## chapter one

1. C. Goodenow and E.L. Gaier, "Best Friends: The Close Reciprocal Friendships of Married and Unmarried Women" (Unpublished paper, 1990).

2. Arlie Russell Hochschild, "Emotion Work, Feeling Rules, and Social Structure," *American Journal of Sociology* 85 (1979): 551–75.

3. Stacey J. Oliker, *Best Friends and Marriage: Exchange Among Women* (Berkeley: University of California Press, 1989).

4. Ibid., 125–26.

5. Anastasia Toufexis, "Coming from a Different Place," *Time,* Fall 1990, 64–65.

6. Ibid.

## chapter three

1. Connie Marshner, *Can Motherhood Survive? A Christian Looks at Social Parenting* (Brentwood, Tenn.: Wolgemuth and Hyatt, 1990), 31.

2. Jennie Dimkoff, "Choosing to Trust," cassette available from 133 W. Maple Street, Fremont, MI 49412.

3. "The American Mother: A Landmark Survey for the 1990s," *Ladies Home Journal,* May 1990, 136.

4. Lee Ezell, *The Missing Piece* (Toronto: Bantam Books, 1988), 67.

5. Ibid., 69.

6. Gloria Gaither, ed, *What My Parents Did Right* (Nashville: Star Song, 1991), 226.

7. Foster Cline, "Understanding and Treating the Severely Disturbed Child."

8. Gaither, *What My Parents Did Right,* 217.

9. Ibid., 218.

10. Recommended reading from Carolyn Koons:
    *Healing Life's Hurts,* Dennis Linn and Matthew Linn
    *Healing for Damaged Emotions,* David Seamands
    *The Gift of Inner Healing,* Ruth Carter Stapleton
    *Making Peace with Your Past,* H. Norman Wright

## chapter four

1. L.M. Montgomery, *Anne of Green Gables* (Toronto: Bantam Books, 1981), 87.
2. Jacqueline Sachs, *Language, Gender, and Sex in Comparative Perspective* (Cambridge: Cambridge University Press, 1987), 178–88.
3. Sydney Taylor, *All-of-a-Kind Family* (Chicago: Follett Publishing Company, 1951), 58.
4. Deborah Tannen, *You Just Don't Understand: Men and Women in Conversation* (New York: William Morrow and Company, 1990), 35.
5. Ibid., 249.
6. Louisa May Alcott, *Little Women* (New York: Dilithium Press, Ltd., 1987), 3.
7. Tania Aebi, "Go Away, Little Girl," *Mademoiselle,* April 1990, 227.

## chapter five

1. Elizabeth Fishel, *Sisters* (New York: Quill, 1979), 39.
2. Ann Kiemel Anderson and Jan Reim, *Struggling for Wholeness* (Nashville: Thomas Nelson, 1986), 37.
3. Anne Ortlund as quoted by Jeanne Hendricks in *A Mother's Legacy* (Colorado Springs: NavPress, 1988), 38.
4. Delois Barrett Campbell as quoted by Roxanne Brown in "Sister Love," *Ebony,* September 1989, 29.
5. Laura B. Randolph, "How Sisters Deal with the Fame of Their Sisters," *Ebony,* December 1991, 110, 112.
6. Fishel, *Sisters,* 29.

## chapter six

1. Stephen P. Bank and Michael D. Kahn, *The Sibling Bond* (New York, Basic Books, 1982), 57.
2. Ibid., 57.
3. Gary Smalley and John Trent, *The Blessing* (Nashville: Thomas Nelson, 1986), 17.
4. Elizabeth Fishel, *Sisters* (New York: Quill, 1979), 1.
5. Tara Markey as quoted by Dan Morris in "Mom Liked You

Best: How Christians Outgrow Sibling Rivalry," *U.S. Catholic,*
January 1989, 9.
6. Ann Kiemel Anderson and Jan Reim, *Struggling for Wholeness* (Nashville: Thomas Nelson, 1986), 17.
7. Ibid., 18.
8. Karen Mains, "Don't Give Me That Guilt Trip" (Wheaton, Ill.:
Chapel of the Air, tape 648a).

**chapter seven**
1. Lillian Rubin, *Just Friends* (New York: Harper and Row,
1985), 188.

**chapter eight**
1. Rubin, *Just Friends* (New York: Harper and Row, 1985), 188.
2. Kathie Lee Gifford, *I Can't Believe I Said That!* (New York:
Pocket Books, 1992), 272.
3. P. O'Connor, "Women's Confidantes Outside Marriage:
Shared or Competing Sources of Intimacy?" *Sociology* 25:
2:241–54.

**chapter nine**
1. Ann Cryster, *The Wife-in-law Trap* (New York: Pocket Star
Books, 1990), 30.
2. Ibid., 2.
3. Ibid., 15–16.
4. Ibid., 145.
5. Glynnis Walker, *Solomon's Children* (New York: Arbor House,
1986), 152.
6. Ibid., 153.
7. Ibid.
8. Larry Richards, *The Bible Reader's Companion* (Wheaton, Ill.:
Victor, 1991), 42.
9. Cryster, *The Wife-in-law Trap,* 31.

**chapter ten**
1. Paul E. Little, *How to Give Away Your Faith,* cassette (Costa
Mesa, Calif.: OneWay Library, 1973).